Advance Praise For

After Empire: Myth, Rhetoric, and Democratic Revival

"*After Empire* chronicles America's addiction to war-in-the-name-of-peace, wherein the military-industrial complex entwines with crippling national mythologies. Drs. Ivie and Giner argue that by seeing the world as a series of threats, our imaginations have shriveled, leaving us rotating from self-righteous exceptionalism to other-fearing doubts. Moving past that dynamic, the authors plot a "passage to democracy," where the nation grows out of imperial hubris and into mature, deliberative democracy."

—Stephen J. Hartnett
Professor, Department of Communication, University of Colorado, Denver

"In *After Empire: Myth, Rhetoric, and Democratic Revival*, Robert L. Ivie and Oscar Giner unpack the way that contemporary American myths of war have played a role in legitimizing war and creating an American empire built around a militarized society. They show that creation of an alternative mythology privileging dissent is essential to rebuilding American democracy. The book is cogently argued, based on groundbreaking research on myth and militarism, and a genuine pleasure to read!"

—Robert C. Rowland
Professor, Department of Communication Studies, University of Kansas

"*After Empire* offers both an analysis of contemporary US war culture and an intervention into it in the hope of making the US a healthier democracy. Focusing on the intersection of politics, popular culture, and myth, and deftly integrating theory, method, and substantive content, Ivie and Giner provide a map of the current US public sphere in ways that will interest academics as well as practitioners and prove useful for courses in rhetoric, history, and political science."

—Mary E. Stuckey, Edwin Erle Sparks
Professor of Communication Arts & Sciences, Pennsylvania State University, University Park

After Empire

Mitchell S. McKinney and Mary E. Stuckey
General Editors

Vol. 51

Robert L. Ivie and Oscar Giner

After Empire

Myth, Rhetoric, and Democratic Revival

PETER LANG
New York · Berlin · Bruxelles · Chennai · Lausanne · Oxford

Library of Congress Cataloging-in-Publication Data

Names: Ivie, Robert L., author. | Giner, Oscar, 1953- author.
Title: After empire: myth, rhetoric, and democratic revival / Robert L. Ivie, Oscar Giner.
Description: New York: Peter Lang, [2024] | Series: Frontiers in political communication, 1525-9730; vol. 51 | Includes bibliographical references and index.
Identifiers: LCCN 2023055924 (print) | LCCN 2023055925 (ebook) | ISBN 9781636678474 (hardback) | ISBN 9781636675480 (paperback) | ISBN 9781636675497 (ebook) | ISBN 9781636675503 (epub)
Subjects: LCSH: Rhetoric–Political aspects–United States–History–21st century. | Political culture–United States–History–21st century. | Obama, Barack–Oratory. | Strategic culture–United States. | United States–Foreign relations–2009-2017. | Democracy–United States.
Classification: LCC P301.5.P67 I95 2024 (print) | LCC P301.5.P67 (ebook) | DDC 808.5/1–dc23/eng/20240223
LC record available at https://lccn.loc.gov/2023055924
LC ebook record available at https://lccn.loc.gov/2023055925
DOI 10.3726/b21656

Bibliographic information published by the Deutsche Nationalbibliothek. The German National Library lists this publication in the German National Bibliography; detailed bibliographic data is available on the Internet at http://dnb.d-nb.de.

Cover design by Peter Lang Group AG

ISSN 1525-9730 (print)
ISBN 9781636675480 (paperback)
ISBN 9781636678474 (hardback)
ISBN 9781636675497 (ebook)
ISBN 9781636675503 (epub)
DOI 10.3726/b21656

© 2024 Peter Lang Group AG, Lausanne
Published by Peter Lang Publishing Inc., New York, USA
info@peterlang.com—www.peterlang.com

All rights reserved.
All parts of this publication are protected by copyright.
Any utilization outside the strict limits of the copyright law, without the permission of the publisher, is forbidden and liable to prosecution.
This applies in particular to reproductions, translations, microfilming, and storage and processing in electronic retrieval systems.

This publication has been peer reviewed.

To Eric and Sara, my son and my daughter, both near and dear.
RLI

For Sara, Manuel, and Jimena
for Atticus, little Arthur, and beautiful Inés
OG

CONTENTS

Introduction	1
Chapter 1 At the Threshold	16
Chapter 2 Incantations of Empire	38
Chapter 3 Veteran's Lament	62
Chapter 4 Abraham's Angels	82
Chapter 5 Passage to Democracy	108
Selected Bibliography	135
Notes on Authors	149
Index	151

INTRODUCTION[1]

Yet soul be sure the first intent remains, and shall be carried out,
Perhaps even now the time has arrived.

Walt Whitman, "Passage to India"[2]

The people of the United States are trapped in the mythology of war. At the beginning of the twenty-first century, a legacy of Indian war, revolutionary war, frontier war, civil war, imperial war, world war, and cold war culminated in an open-ended war on terror. Militarism molded the national identity into a patriotic ethos of moral supremacy, advanced weaponry, and global dominion. It circumscribed the nation's sense of reality, including what citizens believed to be the actual state of world affairs, and restricted what they thought could and should be changed. The so-called "Forever War" on terrorism eventually morphed into what Karen J. Greenberg called "the era of Eternal War" in which a proxy war in Ukraine too easily could turn into a direct confrontation between nuclear superpowers, geopolitical tensions with China might break out into war over Taiwan or elsewhere, and ongoing frictions with Iran, North Korea, and Syria could escalate, even as the continuing war on terrorism was refocused on Africa. War had become "ever more accepted as a permanent condition."[3] Living in anything but a state of war was nearly unthinkable, at least for the foreseeable future.

A mindset of exceptionalism—the mythic sensibility of a savior nation exempted from normal constraints on war making—masked an imperial hubris that rendered the country always insecure in an alien world of perceived evildoers. Empire's war culture was sustained by a deeply embedded and ritually enacted devil myth and outward projections of evil. It reduced democracy to a rationalization for war. Democracy became something to contain and defend rather than practice.[4] The prospect of democratic life in imperial America was reduced to fantasy.[5]

"Yet soul be sure," the exigency of the times is to carry out a people's first intent. *After Empire* operates on the terrain of political myth, not to debunk myth but to engage it on its own terms. It assumes that myth is the stuff of political life, that myth molds a people's sense of reality, that it carries a potentiality for cultural renewal, but that taking language literally ensnares us in myth's artifices. "Myth is about the sacred," Robert Rowland affirms, and thus provides a people with a source of transcendence and identity. Purpose can be found in myths "perceived as both true and sacred," but they can become inflexible and due for a retelling.[6]

War culture, as defined by Kelly Denton-Borhaug, is a lethal example of a naturalized and inflexible discursive formation. It is nothing short of "the normalized interpenetration of the institutions, ethos and practices of war with ever-increasing facets of daily human life ... including the economy, education, diverse cultural sites, patterns of labor and consumption, and even the capacity for imagination." The discourse of militarism synchronizes a society's attitudes and institutions with military goals.[7] War, Adam Hodges observes, is a culturally embedded construct mediated by discourse that creates enemies, mobilizes fighting forces, and structures memories to glorify and mythologize war.[8] The U.S. is hooked on war, as Tom Englehardt insists, to the point of becoming a warrior state.[9]

Ira Chernus examines the rhetorical genesis of the premise of national insecurity as a work of myth. In the twentieth century, he observes, the premise emerged when Franklin Roosevelt recast the defense of the homeland into a universal project of protecting civilization from evil forces. The myth, rhetorically adapted to the immediate circumstances of 1940, solidified over time, shifting the political culture profoundly toward militarism and a state of constant readiness for war. War was no longer perceived as a temporary aberration. A dualistic morality and presumption of national innocence mythically pitted the U.S. against a ubiquitous cast of evildoers and positioned it always on the brink of extinction.[10] The pattern extended to domestic political warfare in which, as Patricia Roberts-Miller observes, "the mask of war" transitioned into a deadly culture war that marks contemporary politics. Cold War anti-communism, she explains, was repurposed by partisan demagogues to demonize policy differences and render political opponents in apocalyptic terms as a satanic force at war with Christianity.[11]

When ensnared in a cultural code, as Lewis Hyde observes, we must have the wit to make our way anew, using "the materials at hand" to shape the story we inhabit.[12] Accordingly, *After Empire* draws on the archetypal image of Old Man Coyote to slip out of the trap of the war myth and revitalize the prospect of democracy. The book summons the mythic spirit of trespass to maneuver through the landscape of empire's dead metaphors. It is a mythopoetic work of prophecy, a kind of trickster howl exposing a literalized human creation to the possibility of change, seeking "the pores of artifice," as Hyde puts it, to reveal a plenitude out of which something new might emerge.[13] It is a predication of possibility as a precondition of change rather than a prediction of what actually will come about.

The book probes the mythic underpinnings of U.S. war culture, asking how they might be reconfigured to foster a culture more conducive to peace. War culture is coextensive with political culture. Working toward a culture of peace under exigent circumstances is crucial to the broader pursuit of democratic values. Without an abatement of war culture, the death throes of empire portend a toxic reign of militarism and authoritarianism.

We address the problem of war culture in the spirit of what Joseph Campbell calls "creative mythology." The mythic motifs of the past, Campbell argues, might be employed in the present for "reasonable ends." While formations of myth inherited from the past often suppress innovation, Campbell believes the creative powers of symbolization in any given case might overcome the constraint of orthodoxy. "Living myth," he calls it, might be received uncoerced to evoke the energy of aspiration when the coercive force of orthodoxy has driven society to a point of no return.[14]

Creative mythology springs not from "the dicta of authority, but from the insights, sentiments, thought, and vision" of individuals who venture forth to shatter and reintegrate "the fixed, already known, in the sacrificial creative fire." The creative act occurs in an illuminating "moment of aesthetic arrest." Its unifying theme is a transcendent archetypal idea rendered in culturally inflected terms. The response it evokes, its social efficacy, depends on how well its message is communicated by symbols both familiar and novel. Such is the "waking power" of suggestive mythological symbols.[15]

Speaking to the generative potential of Robin Diangelo's metaphor of white fragility, Michael Eric Dyson observes that: "It is not enough to be a rhetorician and a semiotician to deconstruct and demythologize whiteness.

One must be a magician of the political and the social, an alchemist of the spiritual and psychological, too."[16] The cultural alchemy of transforming racism is not unlike the process of critically engaging war culture immersed in the creative powers of symbolization.

After Empire's mythopoetic intervention functions rhetorically as a practice of productive criticism.[17] It probes the naturalized metaphors of empire and the discursive instability of war's cultural hegemony to locate a passage into democratic space. Its mythic interpretation of entrapment and escape—of the tyranny of war and possibility of a democratic exodus—is rhetorical criticism conceived as a productive symbolic act of cultural critique. It aims to rework a troublesome formation and tap into democracy's discursive capacity for constructing a more inclusive and less belligerent polity.

Transitioning into democratic space is a step taken toward the development of a culture of peace. "Warism" is Duane Cady's term for the presumption of war, the belief that war is morally justifiable and that peace is acceptable only if it is advantageous to war. The presumption of a culture of peace is that conflict can be managed nonviolently, that peace should be achieved and maintained by peaceful means. It conceives of positive peace as a condition conducive to human fulfillment, an absence not only of military violence but also of the structural violence of human exploitation. It involves an increased appreciation of diversity, equitable wealth sharing, environmental sustainability, and a sense of interdependence, all of which entails democratic visions, values, and practices.[18]

Old Man Coyote

The book's passage to democracy begins by conjuring up the mythic spirit of Old Man Coyote.

INTRODUCTION

Figure: *Coyote at the River*, by Jeff Thomson. Painting reproduced by permission from Jeff Thomson.

In Navajo folklore, Old Man Coyote is the child of the four directions and one of the Twelve Holy People. He created the Milky Way by throwing a fistful of shining pebbles against the night sky after he became tired of pinning stars on Sky one by one. He is the Promethean mediator who stole fire from the Holy People and gave it to First Man and First Woman.

Old Man Coyote is an archetype, hiding unseen in the heart of the forest. This Coyote we see before us, anxiously waiting to cross the river-threshold of consciousness, is his emanation. He inspects the frozen surface of the stream, sniffing the cold wind and listening to the sounds of the winter landscape. He yips to be invited across. He yearns for the priestess to perform her dance, for the sacred clowns of the nation to bridge him across the river through funny actions. He longs to share the blessings that come from the truth spoken by the Thunder Beings of the West. As Simon Ortiz has taught us, "You know, Coyote/is in the origin and all the way/through … he's the cause/of the trouble, the hard times/that things have … /Yet, he came so close/to having it easy./But he said,/Things are just too easy…."[19]

Coyote is a shaggy, shiftless transgressor. He is the troublemaker who relies on cleverness, humor, and deception to disturb sacrosanct ways of thinking and being. He is a trope of cultural fluidity and an antidote to an excessive fear of otherness. Coyote reminds us that all cultural categories produce dirt, which consists of elements or associations left out, left over, excreted, abstracted, or disposed of to achieve a seemingly more perfect order. He is often symbolically killed while trespassing sacred boundaries but never actually dies.

Cultural categories can be codified and institutionalized by purging or ignoring details that otherwise would render them unstable. In U.S. political culture, democracy is such a cultural category. Drained of political import and ideologically rigidified into a pretext for war, democracy is ever reduced to an empty promise, the vigorous and intensive practice of which is perpetually deferred. It is not perceived as a political practice for the here and now.

Coyote—who is wild and often mangy—works with a pure heart: his purpose is that of life itself. He is the agent of the Holy Spirit in its creative, evolutionary labor. Coyote is a shape-shifter: he must impact the world through the work of sacred clowns, alchemists, and sometimes, through the efforts of performative critics. With mournful laughter, he liberates petrified vitality.

Coyote's alchemy is outlawed by ruling classes who wish to conserve their fading power, and by those who guard—like decaying dragons—their medieval pile of gold. Coyote's grin can be perceived in the triumphal face of the Savior who freed imprisoned souls from the Dungeon of Original Sin, and in the visages of the grim *citoyens* who stormed the Bastille to create a New Order at the turn of the eighteenth century. In his heart—possessed by Spirit—Coyote howls like a father grieving the death of his son, and yells like a child freed from school by the arrival of summer days: "Burn this edifice down!"

Americans have become accustomed to a distrust of democracy, a distrust grounded in a mythic fear of irrationality and disorder.[20] Distempered democracy, contained and suppressed, is an internal demon, an "other" lurking within the body politic, which exaggerates the nation's sense of domestic and foreign endangerment. Cultural tricksters would disrupt projections of insecurity. Lewis Hyde remarks:

> Trickster isn't a run-of-the-mill liar and thief. When he lies and steals, it isn't so much to get away with something or get rich as to disturb the established categories of truth and property and, by so doing, open the road to possible new worlds.[21]

Tricksters perform the essential function of keeping concepts from becoming calcified and reified. They cross over ideological boundaries, violate decorum, and pilfer cultural symbols to create ambiguity and produce ambivalence. The rhetorical vocation of democratic tricksters is to discover hidden openings in the dividing walls that bedevil us.

Mythic Interventions

After Empire offers an approach to U.S. war culture that operates at the intersection of critical discourse studies, where scholars of rhetoric, politics, and public culture converge. Its concern with democracy and the transformation of U.S. war culture and its focus on political myth speak to interdisciplinary interests. As a work of mythic intervention and an extension of the method of productive rhetorical criticism, it positions the scholar as rhetor, that is, as cultural observer and cultural agent. Its outlook is prognostic. It envisions a movement out of war culture by way of democratic dissent.

The book resonates with the kind of performative scholarship found, for example, in David Campbell's work on writing security, in which he examines discourses of culture and identity to reorient U.S. foreign policy. Campbell's commitment is to re-writing U.S. security. Thus, he quotes approvingly Michel Foucault's observation that "practicing criticism is a matter of making facile gestures difficult."[22] Campbell's interest in biopolitics treats scholarly critique as political and cultural resistance to the spectacle of security. Toward that end, he faults the contemporary discourse of photojournalism of war in Afghanistan for its lack of critical purchase on the normalized "writing of political space."[23] Likewise, Marouf Hasian Jr. undertakes a genealogical critique of the reified discourse of drone warfare, a discourse that plays on the myth of national innocence and fantasy of clean warfare. He interrogates mythic metanarratives, including clinical images of precision targeting, from which Americans develop arguments to justify the use of weaponized drones—a "drone syndrome," he observes, of arguments that fall on deaf ears outside the confines of U.S. political culture.[24]

After Empire is congruent with engaged research in multiple scholarly venues. John Paul Lederach envisions scholarship as a creative act that performs the art of building peace. His work is about watching for metaphors as cultural resources to mobilize the moral imagination.[25] Rhetorical critic Michael Butterworth investigates the mythology and rituals of baseball as a cultural force that undermines democracy in the U.S. and is complicit in the Manichean topos of post-9/11 war discourse.[26] Stephen Hartnett works at the intersection of rhetoric and political theory to analyze and act against the discursive formation of militarism.[27] Political theorist Ernesto Laclau, aiming to advance popular democracy, turns to rhetoric for a model of how metaphor and other tropes can articulate a working foundation for managing antagonism constructively while pursuing progressive social action.[28]

Working in the field of philosophy and ethics, Andrew Fiala undertakes a critical genealogy of the Just War doctrine, exposing the myths and memes of American exceptionalism in order to shift the cultural presumption more toward peace, or practical pacifism, and away from war.[29] Literary scholar, Donald E. Pease, critiques the contemporary iteration of mythic American exceptionalism in its cultural spectacle and tragic extension to foreign policy.[30] Historian Andrew Bacevich dons the cap of the realist, channeling Reinhold Niebuhr (pastor, theologian, author, activist) to critique post-9/11 U.S. imperialism and its commitment to global war on terror as an affliction of U.S. culture, politics, and economics. A determination to remake the world in the country's own image, an ingrained self-adulation and sense of entitlement, he prophesizes, constitutes an irrational and self-defeating penchant for perpetual war, a fool's errand of imperial delusion that is oblivious to an approaching day of reckoning.[31]

These and other projects of cultural intervention in the field of critical inquiry render *After Empire*'s particular approach and contribution legible in a multidisciplinary context. Its mythic intervention in American culture is foreshadowed in several exemplary models. In his *Studies in Classic American Literature*, D.H. Lawrence, a celebrated myth maker himself, extracts foundational American myths from the classic literature of pre-eminent American writers. William Carlos Williams' *In the American Grain* tries to "re-name the things seen, now lost in the chaos of borrowed titles ... under which the true character lies hid." Williams brings "a poetic imagination to the task of reconstructing a live tradition for Americans." Richard Slotkin's admired trilogy (*Regeneration through Violence*, *The Fatal Environment*, and *Gunfighter Nation*) delineates the cultural and political manifestations of the myth of the American frontier throughout the nation's history.[32] If myths are, as Slotkin suggests, the "intelligible mask" of the "national character," then re-examination, identification. and re-formulation of foundational myths are a conduit to rediscovering America's democratic self.

The scholarly milieu of *After Empire* is cultural discourse studies, which consists of critical works responsive to contemporary challenges, including the challenge of U.S. hegemony in an era of accelerated globalization and global warfare. Shi-xu conceptualizes cultural discourse studies as "an alternative mode of research in service of the cultural politics of coexistence." It is an overarching paradigm that encompasses various critical sub-paradigms and modes of intervention. Critical discourse researchers seek to discover and demystify ethnocentric constructs, raise critical consciousness, and promote intellectual creativity.[33]

Various recent books related to U.S. discourses of war and peace fit under the broad umbrella of cultural discourse studies. Marouf Hasian and his colleagues critically engage the mythos of contemporary U.S. war discourse from the rhetorical perspective of argumentation.[34] Heather Ashley Hayes' critical analysis of the U.S. drone program shows how rhetoric and violence travel together in the global war on terror to rearticulate subjectivities and situations.[35] Andrea Greenbaum reveals how war is culturally appropriated, how it invades the public imagination to permeate television, film, literature, and fashion. Stephen Heidt shows how U.S. presidential end-of-war rhetoric, operating under the sign of peace, rehabilitates the war-justifying trope of savagery to reinforce war culture.[36] Transforming war culture is an ongoing project to which *After Empire* contributes mythopoetic perspective.[37] As Sheila Kennedy observes, a conflicted people living together in democratic community requires a "culturally endorsed mythos" for deliberating their "deep and inevitable differences."[38]

Preview

Our story of U.S. empire unfolds in five chapters. In Chapter 1, Coyote ventures to the edge of war culture. Barack Obama's arrival on the presidential scene promises a change in the nation's mindset of war. He would reform the myth of American exceptionalism by democratizing it, but he soon encounters relentless resistance to his initiatives, which force him to play the role of reluctant warrior and rhetorical juggler. By locating Obama's mixed identity within the larger cultural history of hemispheric America, we can see more clearly that he embodies a change that threatens the traditional privilege of white exceptionalism. In the eyes of the living descendants of European colonizers, black Obama is an illegitimate ruler—in Shakespearean terms, a modern Caliban who, having appropriated Prospero's books of magic, bestirs the tempest of America's continental soul. His presence in the White House foretells an end of empire that would bend the arc of history.

In Chapter 2, Coyote traverses the landscape of dead metaphors that render empire the natural order of things. The necessity of war is signified by ritually depicting it as rhythmical, timeless, migratory, clean, and heroic. As its symbolic order rigidifies, empire defies critique, leaving it increasingly disposed to an eruption of violence and authoritarianism. The outburst of Donald Trump's apocalyptic demagoguery signals empire's impending collapse.

In Chapter 3, Coyote assumes the mask of the warrior, which symbolizes patriotism, courage, sacrifice, and faith in the nation's sacred mission. Military veterans advocating for peace appropriate the mythic authority of the soldier, ancient and contemporary. The incongruity of veteran combatants opposing U.S. militarism creates an opening for critique. The prophetic voice of warriors waging peace directs attention to the evil of war, distorted images of the enemy, the confluence of militarism, racism, and injustice, and constructive alternatives for reconciling differences. The warrior's critique prefigures a possibility of change. Like ancient rumors trapped in a cultural heritage, veteran voices call out from a magic well of lived experiences. They cross over settled conceptual boundaries to intermix war and peace, claiming the knowledge of war-fighting for the task of peacemaking.

In Chapter 4, Coyote leads us beyond the realm of adaptation, adjustment, and correction to the figure of the angel, the mythic source of inspiration, vision, and redirection—the guiding star of genesis. Angel symbolizes new awareness, recognition, and understanding. It is the emblem of revelation. A new god is imagined in the Biblical story of Abraham on the verge of sacrificing Isaac. Here we meet three angels that reveal a new conscience, nurture it, and clear a pathway to its realization. These archetypal figures are Gabriel, Raphael, and Michael in their Biblical manifestation, but Abraham's angels represent mythic sources of symbolic reformulation and renewal on a broad cultural scale and in diverse forms. They are archetypal topoi, cultural sources of rhetorical invention, vehicles for locating and recalling cultural beliefs and values buried within the soul of a people. Here we see how humans become conversant with angels, how at the point of national crisis, an Abraham Lincoln conjures "the better angels of our nature."[39] Angel is precursor of action, bringing about a reversal of fortunes, a divestiture of empire, and a new beginning for democracy.

In Chapter 5, Coyote leads us to the river crossing where, guided by our better angels, we might escape the undemocratic imperial mindset of war and seek the revival of a democracy in critical decline. We cross into a democratic space of interdependence, making connections between peacebuilding and other complementary movements for gender equality, racial justice, environmental protection, and economic wellbeing. Exiting from empire's lethal orthodoxy is democracy's vital prospect. A hybrid discourse of deliberative dissent is the proffered vehicle of democratic renewal and exodus from war culture and thus the object of mythic vision, political conception, and rhetorical illustration in the figure of prosopopoeia.

This, in brief outline, is our critical intervention, the story we tell to break the spell of empire and escape the trap of endless warfare. The story's recurring theme progresses in suspended time, moving successively closer to the moral corollary of the journey. The period of after-empire entwines past, present, and future time at the turning point of cultural renewal. Creative mythology is our modus operandi of rhetorical and cultural critique, aesthetic arrest, and symbolic awakening, which takes us from motifs of initiative, resistance, and lament to images of revelation and passage, culminating in a democratic discourse of deliberative dissent. This is our invitation to share in the journey and our aspiration for it to carry onward.

Notes

1. A segment of this chapter is drawn from Robert L. Ivie and Oscar Giner, "Old Man Coyote and the In-Between," *China Media Research* 11, no. 2 (2015): 85–92.
2. Walt Whitman, "Passage to India," in *Leaves of Grass: First and "Death-bed" Editions*, ed. Karen Karbiener (New York: Barnes and Noble Classics), 553.
3. Karen J. Greenberg, "Will It Never Stop? From Forever War to Eternal War," *TomDispatch*, April 11, 2023, https://tomdispatch.com/will-it-never-stop/. On the high level of tensions between China and the U.S., for example, Thomas Friedman observed "both countries have so demonized the other" that "the smallest misstep by either side [over Taiwan] could ignite a U.S.-China war that would make Ukraine look like a neighborhood dust-up" (Thomas L. Friedman, "What Are America and China Fighting About, Anyway?" *New York Times*, April 14, 2023, https://www.nytimes.com/2023/04/14/opinion/china-america-relationship.html). Earlier in the year, Four-Star U.S. General Mike Minihan predicted that the U.S. and China could be at war in 2025 (Charlie Campbell, "U.S. General's Prediction of War with China 'in 2025' Risks Turning Worst Fears into Realty," *Time*, January 31, 2023, https://time.com/6251419/us-china-general-war-2025/). And by May 2023, *Time* reported that, according to the Pentagon, the arms supply mission to Ukraine already was "the largest transfer of arms in history from the U.S. military to a foreign nation": W. J. Hennigan, "Arsenal of Democracy: The Race to Arm Ukraine," *Time* nos. 17–18 (May 8/May 15, 2023): 32.
4. Robert L. Ivie and Oscar Giner, *Hunt the Devil: A Demonology of US War Culture* (Tuscaloosa: University of Alabama Press, 2015). See also, Robert L. Ivie, "Democracy and Militarism," in *The Marketing of War in the Age of Neo-Militarism*, ed. Kostas Gouliamos and

Christos Kassimeris (New York: Routledge, 2012), 87–106. For a study of how "founding fictions" marginalized the U.S. citizenry, even in the name of promoting democracy, see Jennifer R. Mercieca, *Founding Fictions* (Tuscaloosa: University of Alabama Press, 2010).

5 The symptoms of democracy's decline in the U.S. are addressed in Freedom House's 2022 report, summarized by Sara Repucci, "Reversing the Decline of Democracy in the United States," *Freedom House*, n.d., https://freedomhouse.org/report/freedom-world/2022/global-expansion-authoritarian-rule/reversing-decline-democracy-united-states, accessed April 19, 2023. "American democracy is dying," observes Brian Klass, "America's Self-Obsession Is Killing Its Democracy," *The Atlantic*, July 21, 2022, https://www.theatlantic.com/ideas/archive/2022/07/american-democracy-breakdown-authoritarianism-rise/670580/.

6 Robert C. Rowland, "Obama's Rhetoric of Myth and Reason," in *Reconsidering Obama: Reflections on Rhetoric*, ed. Robert E. Terrill (New York: Peter Lang, 2017), 54–5.

7 Kelly Denton-Borhaug, *U.S. War Culture, Sacrifice and Salvation* (Oakville, CT: Equinox Publishing, 2011), 15. For a reasonably comprehensive definition of war culture, see Anthony J. Marsella, "The United States of America: 'A Culture of War,'" *International Journal of Intercultural Relations* 35, no. 6 (2011): 714–28. The nation's ingrained habit of war, in Marsella's terms, is a culture "characterized by a complex socialization process that moves from beliefs and assumptions about what is right, correct, and good (i.e., ethos), to important institutions and then to individual and group psyches. Cultures of war thrive on maintaining an ethos and high levels of fear and nationalism to justify war and violence. They claim … that they are bringing democracy, liberation, modernization, and hope to the very people they will subsequently conquer" (pp. 720–1).

8 Adam Hodges, "War, Discourse, and Peace," in *Discourses of War and Peace*, ed. Adam Hodges (New York: Oxford University Press, 2013), 3.

9 Tom Englehardt, *The American Way of War: How Bush's Wars Became Obama's* (Chicago: Haymarket Books, 2010), 1–7.

10 Ira Chernus, "Franklin D. Roosevelt's Narrative of National Insecurity," *Journal of Multicultural Discourses* 11, no. 2 (2016): 135–48. The pattern can be traced farther back in U.S. history. A rhetoric of "enemyship," for example, was deployed by the founders to shift the public mindset from democratic revolutionaries to devout patriots defending their country from its enemies, a development in support of elite rule over democratic governance; see Jeremy Engels, *Enemyship: Democracy and Counter-Revolution in the Early Republic* (East Lansing: Michigan State University Press, 2010).

11 Patricia Roberts-Miller, "The Mask of War and the War of Masks: The Fabricated Culture War Gets Deadly," *Javnost–The Public* 30, no. 1 (2023): 111–27. On the subject of demagoguery as demonization, see Patricia Roberts-Miller, *Demagoguery and Democracy* (2017; New York: The Experiment, LLC, 2020), and Patricia Roberts-Miller, *Rhetoric and Demagoguery* (Carbondale: Southern Illinois University Press, 2019).

12 Lewis Hyde, *Trickster Makes This World: Mischief, Myth, and Art* (New York: North Point Press, 1998), 277–9.

13 Hyde, 292.

14 Joseph Campbell, *The Masks of God: Creative Mythology* (1968; New York: Penguin Compass, 1991), xx, 3–6.

15 Campbell, 6–8, 40, 65 92–4.
16 Michael Eric Dyson, "Foreword," in Robin Diangelo, *White Fragility: Why It's So Hard for White People to Talk About Racism* (Boston: Beacon Press, 2018), x.
17 Productive criticism is an approach to rhetorical criticism that conceives of critique as a culturally engaged practice, i.e., as a rhetorical enactment of public culture. As a mode of cultural critique and intervention, it aims to affirm and construct as well as resist and deconstruct problematic formations, rendering them contestable and subject to reflection and reformulation. It engages democratic culture to enrich the social imaginary for bridging the human divide. See Robert L. Ivie, "Productive Criticism at the Crossroads: Interventions, Trajectories, and Intersections," *Review of Communication* 16, no. 1 (2016): 104–7; and Robert L. Ivie, "Productive Criticism Then and Now," *American Communication Journal* 4, no. 3 (2001), http://ac-journal.org/journal/vol4/iss3/special/ivie.htm.
18 Ivie, "Productive Criticism," 106; Duane Cady, *From Warism to Pacifism: A Moral Continuum* (Philadelphia: Temple University Press, 1989), 3–4; Robert L. Ivie, "Hierarchies of Equality: Positive Peace in a Democratic Idiom," in *The Handbook of Communication Ethics*, ed. George Cheney, Steve May, and Debashish Munshi (New York: Routledge, 2011), 375; Elise Boulding, *Cultures of Peace: The Hidden Side of History* (Syracuse, NY: Syracuse University Press, 2000), 1; Marsella, 714–28; David Cortright, *Peace: A History of Movements and Ideas* (Cambridge: Cambridge University Press, 2008), 6–8; Katerina Standish et al., eds., *The Palgrave Handbook of Positive Peace* (Singapore: Palgrave Macmillan, 2022).
19 Simon Ortiz, *Shaking the Pumpkin*, ed. Jerome Rothenberg (Albuquerque: University of New Mexico Press, 1991), 91.
20 Robert L. Ivie, *Democracy and America's War on Terror* (Tuscaloosa: University of Alabama Press, 2005), 50.
21 Hyde, 13.
22 David Campbell, *Writing Security: United States Foreign Policy and the Politics of Identity*, rev. ed. (Minneapolis: University of Minnesota Press, 1998).
23 David Campbell, "How Photojournalism Has Framed the War in Afghanistan," in *In/visible War: The Culture of War in Twenty-First-Century America*, ed. Jon Simons and John Louis Lucaites (New Brunswick, NJ: Rutgers University Press, 2017), 28.
24 Marouf Hasian Jr., *Drone Warfare and Lawfare in a Post-Heroic Age* (Tuscaloosa: University of Alabama Press, 2016).
25 John Paul Lederach, *The Moral Imagination: The Art and Soul of Building Peace* (New York: Oxford University Press, 2005).
26 Michael Butterworth, *Baseball and Rhetorics of Purity: The National Pastime and American Identity During the War on Terror* (Tuscaloosa: University of Alabama Press, 2010).
27 Stephen John Hartnett and Laura Ann Stengrim, *Globalization and Empire* (Tuscaloosa: University of Alabama Press, 2006).
28 Ernesto Laclau, *The Rhetorical Foundations of Society* (London: Verso, 2014).
29 Andrew Fiala, *The Just War Myth: The Moral Illusions of War* (Lanham, MD: Rowman & Littlefield, 2008).

30   Donald E. Pease, *The New American Exceptionalism* (Minneapolis: University of Minnesota Press, 2009).
31   Andrew J. Bacevich, *The Limits of Power: The End of American Exceptionalism* (New York: Metropolitan Books, 2008).
32   D. H. Lawrence, *Studies in Classic American Literature* (Garden City, NY: Doubleday and Co., 1955); William Carlos Williams, *In the American Grain* (New York: New Directions, 1956), front matter and back cover; the Slotkin volumes are published by University of Oklahoma Press, 1973, 1985, and 1992.
33   Shi-xu, "Cultural Discourse Studies," in *The International Encyclopedia of Language and Social Interaction*, ed. Karen Tracy (Hoboken, NJ: John Wiley and Sons, Inc., 2015), 288–9, 291.
34   In addition to Hasian's *Drone Warfare*, another book examines the myth of exceptionalism and exceptionalist arguments in the long manhunt for Bin Laden: Marouf Arif Hasian, Jr. and Megan D. McFarlane, *Cultural Rhetorics of American Exceptionalism and the Bin Laden Raid* (New York: Peter Lang, 2013). Still another book explores rhetoric's role in the expansion of the national security state after 9/11 as a discourse coproduced by elites and non-elites: Marouf Arif Hasian, Jr., Shawn Lawson, and Megan D. McFarlane, *The Rhetorical Invention of America's National Security State* (Lanham, MD: Lexington Books, 2015).
35   Heather Ashley Hayes, *Violent Subjects and Rhetorical Cartography in the Age of the Terror Wars* (New York: Palgrave Macmillan, 2016).
36   Stephen J. Heidt, *Resowing the Seeds of War: Presidential Peace Rhetoric since 1945* (East Lansing: Michigan State University Press, 2021).
37   For an example of earlier critical work on rhetoric and cultural myth, see Janice Hocker Rushing and Thomas S. Frentz, "Integrating Ideology and Archetype in Rhetorical Criticism," *Quarterly Journal of Speech* 77, no. 4 (1991): 385–406, and Thomas S. Frentz and Janice Hocker Rushing, "Integrating Ideology and Archetype in Rhetorical Criticism, Part II: A Case Study of *Jaws*," *Quarterly Journal of Speech* 79, no. 1 (1993): 61–81.
38   Sheila Kennedy, *God and Country: America in Red and Blue* (Waco, TX: Baylor University Press, 2007), 4–5, 209–10.
39   Abraham Lincoln, *The Portable Abraham Lincoln*, ed. Andrew Delbanco (New York: Penguin Books, 1993), 204.

· 1 ·
AT THE THRESHOLD[1]

The rhetorical phenomenon of Barack Obama arriving on the presidential scene posed a challenge to U.S. political culture, especially in view of his call to change the nation's mindset of war, his reframing of the myth of American exceptionalism, and his commitment to advancing a democratizing metaphor of partnership. He appeared to embody the change he articulated—a possibility his election sanctioned—in professed contrast to his immediate predecessor's militant rhetoric of evil.

Obama contested the mythos of national security by muting the thunderous theme of evil in the 2008 presidential primary and by democratizing the myth of national exceptionalism in the 2008 presidential campaign.[2] The constitutive properties of a discourse of peace were embedded in his presidential rhetoric of change, even though he maintained a studied ambiguity in his rationale for sending additional military personnel to fight in Afghanistan and although the limitations of his metaphor of partnership were manifested in his Nobel Peace Prize acceptance speech.[3] The mixed message in his call for change was the vestige of a rhetorical trickster encountering the limits of cultural transformation.

Obama hit a solid wall of resistance despite his best efforts and his rhetorical acumen. His policy initiatives were met with sheer obstinacy and persistent resistance; his heterodox presidency spawned a strong backlash. One must wonder if the recalcitrance he encountered was a collective exercise in belligerent denial, if the relentless characterization of his foreign policy as soft and indecisive was a symptom of a deeper fear of imperial decline. Certainly, his Republican critics took his democratized conception of American exceptionalism as an affront.[4]

Indeed, the significance of Obama's rhetoric exceeded the insinuation of peace that the guardians of U.S. war culture adamantly rejected. The greater legacy of his presidential discourse, viewed from a mythopoetic perspective, was his juggling of cultural tensions. The democratizing entailments of his rhetorical juggling invoked an allegorical storm of shifting identity that predicated a new America.

Obama's juggling placed him at the cusp of a cultural shift—a movement from the war culture of imperial America toward a new, thickened democracy more committed to positive peace, a turn that reflected his mixed identity within the cultural swell of a broader, hemispheric America. Our account of this prophetic Obama is an exercise, in the words of Michael Kazan, in "storytelling with a political purpose," which fortunately "has not gone out of fashion, the academic rage for explicit theorizing notwithstanding."[5] Let us begin.

Obama's Rhetorical Juggling

Throughout his presidency, Barack Obama straddled the line between warmonger and peacemaker. He was a "reluctant warrior" by columnist Dana Milbank's reckoning. There were "far fewer U.S. troops in harm's way" in his final year than at the start of his presidency, "but to revisit his speeches over the years is to see his journey from hope to hard reality." The journey ended a long way from the aspirations and ideals of the Nobel Peace Prize awarded to him at its beginning.[6] Over 8,000 U.S. troops remained in Afghanistan and almost 5,000 more had been sent back to Iraq.[7]

Straddling, balancing, and juggling are apt tropes for Obama's presidential signature as an advocate for change.[8] Ambiguity and ambivalence surely characterized Obama the reluctant warrior, the rhetorical juggler on issues of war and peace in a time of tension and transition. Juggling conveys the nuance of his discourse, including its mythic vision of democratic exceptionalism. It also gestures to an underlying sensibility that reframes the significance of his presidency, a reframing that helps to see how his tenure in office expanded the meaning of America and to clarify the dogmatic resistance to him as the embodiment of change.

Ambiguity, strategic or otherwise, was the hallmark of Obama's televised speech at West Point on December 1, 2009, a speech in which he explained why he had decided to send 30,000 additional U.S. troops to Afghanistan even as he declared his intention to conclude American involvement in the war. The ambiguity of his purpose was sustained throughout the speech. He insinuated an attitude of peace even as he announced a new war-fighting strategy. He signaled that his administration would be less militant than that of George W. Bush, who had told the West Point cadets a year earlier that the U.S. would stay on the offensive in Afghanistan for as long as it took to win the war. Obama's nuanced discourse kept his options open in a dynamic situation. He paid rhetorical homage to the war gods by declaring the nation was at war even as he embraced the pursuit of peace. He circumscribed foreign policy without abandoning military options. To progressive critics on the left, the speech sounded like more of the same. To conservative critics on the right, it sounded like a retreat from reality. The nation was left in a state of political limbo with the president positioned to fight the war in Afghanistan over a shortened or prolonged timeframe depending on circumstances.[9]

Before and after West Point, Obama's rhetorical ambivalence toward peace displayed constitutive properties for depolarizing U.S. war culture. He resisted a mindset of insidious fear, sheer antagonism, and Manichean oppositions in which U.S. exceptionalism served as the foundational myth of a Pax Americana. He brought to the presidency a discourse of hope and change comprised of democratizing attributes. Even in affirming the present necessity of war, as he did in his Nobel Peace Prize speech, he sustained a delicate balance between the condition of war and the possibility of peace.[10]

The constitutive properties of democratic peacemaking embedded in Obama's nuanced and doubled discourse included hybridity, complementarity, and reflexivity.[11] Hybridity clustered conflicting terms, each with positive connotations, to leverage a potential shift of interpretation. Generating a productive tension between democracy and exceptionalism was a necessary (albeit insufficient) condition for redirecting the national attitude away from militarism and toward peacemaking. Complementarity constituted a relationship of interdependence rather than a transcendence of differences. The composite trope of democratic exceptionalism was neither a leveling figure nor an image of domination but instead a synergic relationship of mutual empowerment through partnership. Obama would restore U.S. primacy by acting more democratically toward the world. Reflexivity converted the energy of the remaining tension between hybrid and complementary terms into an invitation to critical thinking. It turned the discourse productively back upon itself, as when Obama's emphasis shifted between considerations of U.S. primacy and global well-being, alternating between the values of freedom and responsibility, individualism and equality, and exceptionalism and democracy to signal the complexity of a dynamic situation.

Obama adopted a prophetic voice to invoke the myth of U.S. exceptionalism and express national mission in more democratic terms. In the 2008 Democratic Party presidential primaries, he shifted the impulse to mission from a story of moral conquest to a vision of working collaboratively for world peace and social justice. Even as he spoke of the U.S. as the world's last and best hope and affirmed that he would as commander in chief continue to battle evil and spread freedom, he cautioned that all of this must be done in a spirit of partnership mindful of the country's own limitations and imperfections. He straddled the line between making peace and using military force as an instrument of foreign policy—playing the role of the world's reluctant sheriff—to position himself somewhere between a critique of war culture and a defense of the status quo, all the while seemingly inclined toward attenuating the virulent discourse of redemptive violence.[12]

In his election campaign, opposed by Republican John McCain, Obama's prophetic voice inflected exceptionalism with democratic aspirations and embedded democracy in the American dream to advance an attitude of interdependency and collaboration, even as McCain chauvinistically championed a last stand against evil in the war on terror. Obama would fight terrorism by balancing the resort to military force with the initiation of practical diplomacy, working collaboratively with other nations to give more people a stake in the global order. He would emphasize global cooperation over domination. The U.S. remained at the center of Obama's worldview—the greatest country on earth, a shining beacon on a hill, a force of good in the world—but with a more democratic and less pugnacious or crusading outlook. The tension between exceptionalism and democracy—the impulse to supremacy and domination versus an ethic of equality and solidarity—remained precariously balanced and unresolved.[13]

The question of whether and to what degree Obama's rhetorical juggling carried potential for transforming U.S. war culture haunted his Nobel Peace Prize speech. Juggling the theme of peaceful change within the constraints of war culture was tricky business. The potential of an image of partnership and collaboration—which was a democratizing turn on the traditionally messianic narrative of fighting foreign devils—might be enough to befuddle the mindset of war but was insufficient to transform it. The country that believed in its moral exceptionalism would be deprived of convenient scapegoats should it attempt to transcend the demonology of war culture. Thus, Obama deferred to the doctrine of just war and proclaimed that his country must face the reality of the world as it is, where evil exists and, short of a change in human nature, war is required to secure the peace.

Even as Obama accommodated warfare, his gesture to democracy disturbed critics who complained that his foreign policy was soft and indecisive, that it was an exercise in defeatism, that he was managing American decline and giving up on American exceptionalism. Fear of imperial decline sparked a response of militant denial. Straddling the line between war and peace to exercise military restraint, it turned out, was rhetorically prudent of the president. The alternative of overtly acknowledging the end of the American Century would have resulted in political suicide.[14]

Obama's presidency raised the stakes of empire and its war culture. He embodied a changing of the guard that undermined the historical white privilege of exceptionalism. His favorite speech commemorated the fiftieth anniversary of the brutal beating of civil rights marchers in Selma, Alabama. He liked that speech because it expressed so well his view of American exceptionalism.[15] It conveyed the underlying trajectory of his otherwise tenuously balanced presidential rhetoric, a trajectory that would expand the traditionally narrow definition of America. Obama's America was "a constant work in progress." The Selma marchers, who aimed to remake the nation in an image of its democratic ideals, were resisted violently and disparaged as "half breeds," he noted. But bias and discrimination are not immutable, he insisted; racial division was not inherent to his America. "That's what it means to love America. That's what it means to believe in America. That's what it means when we say America is exceptional." To him, being exceptional meant: "We are large, in the words of Whitman, containing multitudes."[16]

Obama channeling Whitman enlarged the American political imaginary, indeed, extended it beyond national boundaries. He bestirred the tempest of America's continental soul. His rhetorical juggling foreshadowed an emergent American character, an expanded and more inclusive sense of the nation replete with all the irresolvable but productive tensions of a robust democracy. This impending increase and augmentation of the nation's democratic self, its recognition and acceptance of multiplicities and complexities, was a faint entailment of Obama's presidential discourse, but his militant critics feared the brewing storm. Their foreboding carried Shakespearian undertones.

The Accession of Caliban

Observe the American continent: it is one and indivisible from Alaska to Patagonia. Columbus did not find Asia and a new passage to the Indies; he encountered a landmass wedged between two oceans in an unknown hemisphere of the world. In our imperial arrogance, we in the United States appropriate the name of the continent to refer to our country; and yet the country, much more than it cares to acknowledge, has been inevitably shaped by the winds of history as they have swept the continent.[17]

In the heart of America lies the Caribbean Sea—the port of entry from Europe and Africa. The sea is guarded by an archipelago named after fantastic islands from medieval cartography: the Antilles. Writing about the Spanish American civilization that developed around the periphery of the Caribbean, José Juan Arrom, the distinguished Cuban analyst of Taíno language and mythology, has advanced the following:

> At first sight one could think that the Caribbean separates those lands, but this is not the case; it unites them culturally. ... The process was begun by Columbus' ships. It was continued by the heavy galleons filled with treasure which tied the main ports of the region with the yarn of their white sails. And also by the slave brigantines, leaving sad, bloody, painful trails with their infamous loads.

In the island of Saint Domingue (formerly Hispaniola, today the island of Haiti and the Dominican Republic), where Columbus founded his original Spanish colony, Native Americans, Europeans, and Africans first confronted each other in the New World:

> The fundamental pattern of their relationship all over the Western Hemisphere—dispossession and extermination of the Indians by the Europeans, who go on to exploit the seized territory with African slave labor—was set for the first time here.

On August 14, 1791, the performance of a voodoo ceremony in Bois Caiman changed the course of American history. A combined army of black slaves and free *mulattoes* fought the first successful slave rebellion in history and forged the first black republic in 1804.[18]

After the execution of Louis XVI in 1793, the European royalist powers declared war against France. When asked by French commanders to join forces against Spain (black Haitians allied with Spain during the early days of the slave uprising), Macaya, an African-born Congolese rebel leader, replied:

> I am the subject of three kings: of the King of the Congo, master of all the blacks; of the King of France who represents my father; of the King of Spain who represents my mother. These three Kings are the descendants of those who, led by a star, came to adore God made man. If I went over to the Republic, I might be forced to make war against my brothers, the subjects of these three kings to whom I have promised loyalty.

In this Caribbean crucible of violence and aspiration for liberty, the *raza* (the Spanish word that would come to mean "the people") was forged, and the mask of a new identity began to take form.[19]

The Haitian slave rebellion had been preceded by numerous slave uprisings in the West Indies, Brazil, and North America. The specter of future successful slave revolts presented an immediate threat to European colonial powers in the New World. Haiti's insurrection created an enduring myth. The dark side of the myth was propagated by French *émigrés* from Saint-Domingue who fled to escape the terror of the uprising: "These exiles brought with them … terrible stories of rape, murder, looting and destruction which were enough to keep Cuban planters from giving an inch to their slaves for nearly a hundred years." Conversely, the revolt perpetuated a shining dream of freedom from colonial rule among American creoles. Haiti gave to history the legendary names of Toussaint Louverture (the name means the Opening), Dessalines, and Christophe. From Haiti in 1815, Simón Bolívar launched his war for the liberation of South America. From Cap Haïtien in 1895, José Martí sailed for death and martyrdom in the war of independence he had organized to free Cuba from Spanish rule.[20]

For the slave colonies in the U.S., events in Haiti proved to be "their worst nightmare made real." But for antebellum black abolitionists, Haiti became a hopeful dream, a beacon that illuminated the path to freedom. In his commencement address at Bowdoin College in 1826, John Browne Russwurm evoked the Haitian revolution:

> On the auspicious day of January first, 1804, [Haitians] declared themselves a free and independent nation. … When once freedom struck their astonished ears, they became new creatures, stepped forth as men, and showed to the world, that though slavery may benumb, it cannot destroy our faculties.

In an obituary column, José Martí once described Henry Highland Garnet as an orator who was heard by Southern runaway slaves "as a Messiah, and was obeyed like Moses." Speaking to the National Negro Convention of 1843 in New York, Garnet called openly for a slave insurrection in the U.S. He evoked the failed revolt of Denmark Vesey in South Carolina in 1822, and linked Vesey's name to a notable list of liberators from the past: "History ... will transcribe his name on the same monument with Moses, Hampden, Tell, Bruce and Wallace, Toussaint L'Ouverture, Lafayette and Washington." At the World's Columbian Exposition in Chicago (1893), the ex-slave, essayist and abolitionist orator Frederick Douglass lectured his audience on "the bearing of [Haiti's] example as a free and independent Republic, upon what may be the destiny of the African race in our own country and elsewhere." Douglass was speaking as co-commissioner of the Haitian Pavilion at its dedication:

> We should not forget that the freedom you and I enjoy today ... the freedom that has come to the colored race the world over, is largely due to the brave stand taken by the black sons of Haiti ninety years ago. ... Striking for their freedom, they struck for the freedom of every black man in the world.

Four hundred years after Columbus' first voyage, on the eve of the U.S. imperial century, Douglass forewarned his audience: "Haiti is black, and we have not yet forgiven Haiti for being black or forgiven the Almighty for making her black."[21]

The election of Barack Obama to the presidency of the United States was like the accession of Caliban to the kingship of his island in Shakespeare's *The Tempest*. Except that in Obama's case, Prospero did not grant Ariel his freedom, or leave the island for Milan. He stayed behind, yielding reluctantly to the rule of the "thing most brutish" (1.2.421) that was once his slave.[22]

The onset of the "American" century was a dislocating event for Spanish American intellectuals. At the outbreak of the Spanish-American war, the Nicaraguan modernist poet Rubén Darío (1867–1916) penned a furious newspaper article:

> I don't want to be on the side of those buffaloes with silver teeth. ... The ideal of those Calibans is confined to the purse and the factory. ... They have temples for all gods but believe in none. ... I cannot be for the triumph of Caliban. ... I who have been on the side of a free Cuba ... am Spain's friend at the moment when I see her attacked by a brutal enemy, which carries violence, power and injustice as its banner.

Darío followed Paul Groussac, who associated the United States and its "unformed calibanesque body" with the half-fish, half-human character of Shakespeare's play. For Darío, Caliban and his monstrous appetites, profane language and lust for power seemed a fitting symbol for a people who "eat, eat again, calculate, drink whisky and make millions."[23]

In 1900, Uruguayan thinker and essayist José Enrique Rodó (1872–1917) published his influential essay *Ariel*, of "long-lasting fame" throughout Spanish America. Rodó's pamphlet took the form of a final address by an old teacher (called Prospero by his students) who invokes Ariel as his inspiration. In Rodó's reading of Shakespeare, Ariel represents "the noble and winged part of the spirit"; superior beings were called to transcend "the tenacious vestiges of Caliban, symbol of clumsiness and sensuality." Ariel was the wind, youth, rationalism, and appreciation of beauty that should guide the youth of America; Caliban was the materialistic society that had developed in the U.S., characterized by "utilitarianism, empty of ideal content, cosmopolitan ambiguity" and "bastard democracy." The fatal flaw of democracy, according to Rodó, was the "ignoble predominance of the number." Popular democratic education must be reformed to focus on the development of an "aristarchy" [*aristarquia*] of morality and culture: "Democracy's affirmation and its glory will consist in eliciting from its bosom, through effective stimuli, the dominion and revelation of true human superiorities." Only then can democracy prevent the "enthronement of Caliban" and the consequent demise of Ariel; only through such means is the soul made ready "for the clear vision of beauty." According to Emir Rodríguez Monegal, "from Rodó on, Caliban was condemned to represent in Latin American letters the worst aspects of democracy: materialism, utilitarianism."[24]

Absent from Rodó's *Ariel* was the consciousness of Black America as a foundational element of American culture. For early European settlers, African languages, religion, and culture were reduced to incomprehensible "drumming, jumping, dancing and singing," or as one Nova Scotia colonizer characterized them, "Negro frolicks." In North America, the slave biographies, spiritual narratives, and nascent African American literature of the nineteenth century proffered undeniable evidence of an African participation in the formulation of an American cultural identity. Phillis Wheatley (1753–84), first African-American woman poet of record, reminded readers that her "sable race" was to be acknowledged:

> Remember, *Christians*, *Negros*, black as *Cain*
> May be refin'd and join th' angelic train.

Plays such as Dion Boucicault's *The Octoroon* (1859) in New York, and Alejandro Tapia y Rivera's *La cuarterona* [*The Quadroon*] (1867) in the Caribbean, reflected a growing acceptance by European Americans of the phenomenon of the mixed-race individual as integral to American society. By the structural prominence given to their heroes, by their implied advocacy and elicited sympathies, these plays suggested that the concept of "American" should expand to include those tainted with African blood. They stopped short of insisting that America does not exist without blackness, or with what a later Caribbean poet would call *négritude*.[25]

Partly inspired in Paris by American *emigrés* from the Harlem Renaissance, the term was first used by Aimé Césaire (1913–2008) in his "Notebook for a Return to my Native Land" (1939). Born in the island of Martinique in the French Caribbean, Césaire was one of the "Three Fathers" of *Négritude*, a philosophical and aesthetic movement that affirmed black pride, history, and heritage in the face of white colonialist Western culture. *Négritude* was a movement in search of a unifying cultural identity for the Black Diaspora. It was "measured by the compass of suffering" produced by the slave trade and European colonialism. Césaire wrote a trilogy of plays on black themes: *The Tragedy of King Christophe* (1963), about the ruler who proclaimed himself King in Haiti after the death of Desssalines; *A Season in the Congo* (1966), about the assassination of Patrice Lumumba; and *A Tempest* (1969), subtitled an "Adaptation of Shakespeare's *Tempest* for a Negro Theater."[26]

In *A Tempest*, Césaire re-defined the inherited symbolic meanings of Shakespeare's characters. Prospero is a banished duke, stripped of power by the Holy Inquisition for magic and sorcery, who was marooned in a "desert isle" with his daughter Miranda. Ariel is a "mulatto slave" in Prospero's service who is willing to compromise in exchange for his eventual freedom; Caliban is a "negro slave" who sings to Shango (the Yoruba god of thunder) and plans violent rebellion against Prospero:

> I know that one day
> my bare fist, just that,
> will be enough to crush your world!
> The old world is crumbling down!

At the end of the play, Prospero frees Ariel, but decides to stay in Caliban's island:

> And now Caliban, it's you and me! ...
> I shall stand firm. ... I shall not let my work perish! I shall protect civilization!

To which Caliban replies with a freedom chant that evokes the Swahili word ("*Uhuru!*") with which he entered in Act One: "LA LIBERTÉ OHÉ, LA LIBERTÉ!"[27]

Shakespeare's audiences were meant to identify with the divine pardon that Prospero granted his betrayers and with the future generation of Italian monarchs (Ferdinand and Miranda) in the play. Following the symbolic associations bestowed by Renan and Fouillée on Shakespeare's characters at the end of the nineteenth century, Rodó had called upon the youth of America to conjure Ariel:

> Ariel is the lofty coronation of Nature's work, which brings to an end, with the flame of the spirit, the ascension of organized forms. Ariel triumphant, means ideality and order in life; noble inspiration of thought, disinterested morals, good taste in art, heroism in action, delicacy in customs. He is the eponymous hero in the epic of the species; he is the immortal protagonist.

But for Césaire, we "savages and men of Inde" (*The Tempest*, 1.2.268), we the blacks and slaves, born on the "still-vexed Bermoothes" (2.2.57) from our mother Sycorax, are the legitimate heirs of our magical islands and fabled continent. We are engaged in an everlasting struggle, in the "agonized womb of consciousness," with our internal Prospero. Putting on the masks of Prospero and Caliban is both an acceptance of the self and the beginning of a search for a cultural identity.[28]

The name Caliban derives from the Taíno voice *caribe*, which Columbus also transcribed as *caníbales* and *caniba* in the *Diary of the First Voyage* (1492–3). The words referred to the Caribs, ferocious inhabitants of the western Antilles "who eat human flesh." Othello's "Cannibals that each other eat,/The Anthropophagi" (*Othello*, 1.3.158–9), have their precursors in John Florio's translation (1603) of Montaigne's essay "On Cannibals" (1580). "There is no doubt at this point," writes Cuban poet and Marxist critic Roberto Fernández Retamar in his important essay "Caliban" (1971), "that *The Tempest* alludes to America, that its island is the mythification of one of our islands."[29]

According to Retamar, Shakespeare's play offers two different visions of America and its natives, both of which were prevalent in Europe during the sixteenth century: (1) the first one is based on Columbus' celebratory accounts of the discovery and the utopian works of Thomas More and Montaigne, which are echoed in the humanist evocation of the Golden Age by Gonzalo after the King of Naples and his retinue wash ashore in *The Tempest*; (2) the second rests on the portrayal of Caliban, an offspring of the "divel," a "savage" who belongs to a "vild race" (1.2.380 and 419–22), which parts from "the typically degraded vision offered by the colonizer of the man he is colonizing." These two revelations are complementary: the first superimposes on foreign lands "projects for political reform that were unrealized in the countries of origin"; the second provides the justification for slavery and genocide.[30]

Retamar calls upon José Martí's "Our America" (1891), one of the seminal essays of Latin American political philosophy, for inspiration. What the "peace of the centuries" required, wrote Martí, was "timely study and the urgent wordless union of the continental soul." In Retamar's view, Martí's concept of "our mestizo [half-breed] America" should be understood as "the distinctive sign of our culture—a culture of descendants, both ethnically and culturally speaking, of aborigines, Africans, and Europeans." He concludes:

> Our symbol then is not Ariel, as Rodó thought, but rather Caliban. ... Prospero invaded the islands, killed our ancestors, enslaved Caliban, and taught him his language to make himself understood. ... What is our history, what is our culture, if not the history and culture of Caliban?[31]

In "Ariel or the agony of a stubborn illusion" (1938), Aníbal Ponce argues that Shakespeare represents his entire epoch in four of the leading figures in *The Tempest*. Successive re-definitions of Caliban oblige continuing symbolic re-definitions of other main characters of the play. Darío explicitly associated the U.S. with Caliban and drew a sharp distinction between the inhabitants of "Brobdingnag" (Swift's land of giants from *Gulliver's Travels*) and those who still conserve "something of the milk of the [Roman] She-Wolf." Prospero was Europe and Spain, from where "a vast cosmopolitan breath will come to help invigorate our own jungle." Miranda, legitimate heir of Prospero's "spiritual grace," was our "Latin soul," which would always prefer Ariel, and never prostitute itself with Caliban.[32]

Rodó assumed the mask of Prospero in his final address to his students. He lectured them in cautionary and inspiring tones—the same ones used by Prospero when speaking to Ferdinand and Miranda after Juno's masque in *The Tempest* (4.1.163–73). America's youth was to identify with the spiritual values of Ariel, inherited from classical Greek civilization and Christianity.

Caliban was "mere will and utility," signified by the "titanic social organism" of the United States at the turn of the century.[33]

For Césaire, Prospero was the European colonizer. Ferdinand and Miranda are the offspring of European civilization; they do not belong to the island and are therefore shipped home by Prospero at the end of Césaire's play. Ariel and Caliban are symbols of Black America, representing not a chasm between spirit and materiality, but rather different tactical approaches in the pursuit of freedom from European colonial rule.

For Retamar, Prospero is the anti-American colonizer. In his Marxist scheme, Shakespeare's magician represents the European-leaning upper classes. Caliban is Oppressed America: the proletarian, aboriginal and former slaves of the New World. Ariel is the lost native intellectual, vacillating between Europe and America, between identification with "metropolitan culture" and that of the "exploited classes."[34]

Juggling meanings and symbolic associations, none of them considered that a single American culture unified the hemisphere.

Obama and the New America

In Chicago on the night Barack Obama was elected president, one could hear in the cheers and delirium of the crowd a sound that was like the blast of Gabriel's trumpet. It came up from the heartland of America, from its deep roots, mighty rivers, dense jungles, and sacred mountains, traversing through its ancient and bloody history. Black and white, pale and colored rejoiced together as if a Yoruba deity had descended upon them, while American flags waved in the autumn evening's air.

Civil rights activist Jesse Jackson struggled to hold back tears that streamed down his cheeks. At Spelman College in Georgia, students danced to the rhythms of hip-hop. At Ebenezer Baptist Church, where Martin Luther King, Jr. once preached, the congregation reveled in amazement as if the Holy Spirit had appeared in its midst. In Harlem streets, people partied as if all the prophecies of the Renaissance had come true, no longer a dream deferred. In Times Square in New York, and in Washington DC before the White House, crowds exulted as if the second coming was at hand.[35]

The world joined in the "Negro frolicks" once derided by a Nova Scotia observer, and everyone romped and gamboled making "a joyful noise unto the Lord" (Psalms 98:4).[36]

Obama had spoken at the Democratic Party convention of 2004, and hearing his voice was "like the penetrance of an apocalyptic wasp":

> I stand here today, grateful for the diversity of my heritage. ... I stand here knowing that my story is part of the larger American story, that I owe a debt to all of those who came before me.

He stood on a platform in Grant Park—named after the general who won the war that gave North American slaves their freedom—and his voice was "as the voice of many waters, and as the voice of a great thunder" (Rev. 14:2):

> Tonight we proved once more that the true strength of our nation comes not from the might of our arms or the scale of our wealth, but from the enduring power of our ideals: democracy, liberty, opportunity and unyielding hope.

Although Obama was a *mulatto*—one of the *gens de couleur* in the racial parlance of Caribbean slavery—he identified as African-American. He spoke in the cadences of old time African-American preachers, echoing the urgency of Frederick Douglass, the eloquence of Martin Luther King, Jr., and the staccato of Malcolm X. "That's how I'm treated," Obama once said, "and that's how I'm viewed. I'm proud of it."[37]

From the island of Haiti, where Négritude first rose to claim its place in the world, to the hallowed halls of U.S. power, the avatar of a New America appeared in the semblance of Caliban. Like Caliban he was born on an island, part of the Pacific archipelago, which had come under U.S. military rule during the Spanish-American war at the dawn of empire. Everyone born on an island has a half-fish, half-human aspect to their nature. (Trying to dispel a misguided tourist's assumption that the young Obama's swimming prowess on the beach was due to his being Hawaiian, his maternal grandfather once clarified: "His mother is from Kansas, his father is from the interior of Kenya, and there isn't an ocean for miles in either damn place.") Like Caliban he was the offspring of *miscegenation*: "The word is humpbacked, ugly, portending a monstrous outcome," Obama wrote in his memoirs. The union of a black man and a white woman was still illegal in a majority of the nation's states when Obama's parents married in 1960.[38]

Future political enemies found easy to believe that like Caliban, Obama was "got by the divel himself." Given the times Obama faced, his father's Muslim heritage implied that his son was a "demi-divel." Obama's mother, who had had the temerity to love a black man, could readily be perceived in the guise of Caliban's "wicked dam," the "foul witch Sycorax," who was banished from Argier and marooned by sailors on Prospero's island for her transgressions. But this Caliban was not a "poisonous slave," but rather a free man who did not curse, or speak in the patois of *creoles*, but in the pristine English of educated Europeans. This "thing of darkness" did not want to rape Miranda and people his island with Calibans, for he was married to a Queen of Sheba (beloved of Salomon) from the South Side of Chicago, who had given birth to two princesses. His given name, Barack, meant "Blessed" in Arabic, and did not originate in legends about the feared cannibals of the Lesser Antilles (*The Tempest*, 1.2.305–81 and 5.1.311–14).

And yet Obama's black ancestry bound him to the "compass of suffering" of Césaire's *négritude*, and his modest upbringing made him a soldier in the "rebellious and glorious ranks" of those oppressed Americans whom Roberto Fernández Retamar had hailed in the name of Caliban.[39]

Back in Hawaii, Obama understood that the black and white worlds he inhabited "each possessed its own language and customs and structures of meaning." But he believed that with some "translation" on his part both worlds "would eventually cohere." Later, in despair at the exacting difficulty of such a transaction, in the dawn of an auspicious morning, he would learn an abiding lesson from the "layers of hurt" and "ragged laughter" of a Billie Holliday song: "Endure—and make music that wasn't there before."[40]

In his "Speech on Race" (entitled "A More Perfect Union") during the Jeremiah Wright controversy, Obama defined the challenges awaiting the nation's future president and expressed the need for the country to "come together." But his call for unity came with an exigency:

> I can no more disown [Jeremiah Wright] than I can disown the black community. I can no more disown him than I can disown my white grandmother. ... These people are a part of me. And they are part of America, this country that I love.

Like Caliban proclaiming his lineage from Sycorax and her god Setebos before a snarling Prospero, he affirmed that his past and heritage would not be left behind:

> I have brothers, sisters, nieces, nephews, uncles and cousins of every race and every hue, scattered across three continents. ... It is a story that has seared into my genetic makeup the idea that this nation is more than the sum of its parts—that out of many, we are truly one.

The multicultural origins of America had never been acknowledged before in such a personal, visceral manner on the threshold of the seat of power of the richest country in the hemisphere.[41]

In his biography of Toussaint Louverture, Madison Smartt Bell records a confrontation between the former Toussaint Bréda and his old slave-master Bayon de Libertat (whom Toussaint cherished) after Louverture became supreme leader of the slave rebellion in Saint Domingue:

> Today there is a greater distance between me and you than there was in the old days between you and me. Return to Habitation Bréda; be firm and just; make the Blacks work well, so that the success of your small interests will add to the general prosperity of the administration of the first of the Blacks, of the General in Chief of Saint Domingue.[42]

But in Obama's time the children of Prospero did not return to their plantations for the prosperity of the nation. Emulating the European powers, which opposed Toussaint's determination to free the slaves, the descendants of European colonizers opposed Obama's initiatives at every turn of his presidency.

Like Louverture, Obama preferred negotiation to outright conflict, but for his detractors he was an illegitimate ruler granted "power, and his seat, and great authority" by the "great dragon," which was "that old serpent, called the Devil, and Satan, which deceiveth the whole world" (Rev. 13.2 and 12.9). By positioning Obama as the Anti-Christ, his opponents framed themselves as the "saints" serving God through the "great tribulation" (Rev. 13.7 and 7.14–15). Congress was the field of battle; the country was Armageddon.[43]

As there was Babylon and New Jerusalem in the Book of Revelation, an old Rome and a new Rome confronting each other in the time of Julius Caesar, an old and a new United States of America in the time of Abraham Lincoln, and an old and new South Africa in the time of Nelson Mandela, Obama was the epic hero of a new Calibanesque America, facing the forces of old Prospero, besieged by the old magician's dated and crumbling empire.

A litany of Obama's achievements during his two terms as president would range from seeing the country through economic recovery to expanding health insurance coverage to the poor, promoting diversity, banning torture, and de-escalating Middle East wars while thawing relations with Cuba. To all this must be added the restoration of gifted political oratory (the sweet songs of Ariel) to the office of president. As he worked on his first political public speech at Occidental College, Obama thought: "With the right words everything could change—South Africa, the lives of ghetto kids just a few miles away, my own tenuous place in the world." By the last year of his presidency, struggling to comfort the families and friends of five police officers fallen in Dallas, he had come to learn the limits of his rhetorical power: "I've seen how inadequate words can be in bringing about lasting change. I've seen how inadequate my own words have been."[44]

When future historians write the story of the Obama presidency, his tenure will be understood as a truly American phenomenon. His actions were symbolic of the ever-present struggle in our hearts: he attempted to forge alchemical gold from the disparate, cultural elements that in the tides of human affairs, came to live in the American continent. He was the new being struggling to be born from an awareness of *négritude* in Aimé Césaire's poem. In a prescient opinion column, Eugene Robinson passed a sober judgment:

> Obama will leave office without having healed the nation's festering racial wounds. He will not have made them worse; rather, he will have allowed us to see how deep they remain and how much healing still needs to take place. It may take years to fully appreciate how dramatically this presidency has bent the arc of history toward justice.

Toussaint did not complete the task of liberating Haitian slaves from European dominance; but as his adopted name (Louverture) implied, he was *the opening* for the liberation of Latin America from European powers and lived as its mythical hero.[45]

The New America—which will include, but will not be ruled by, European frameworks—is half-fish and half-human, and was born through miscegenation from the devil of slavery and the witch of genocide. Obama's rhetorical construction of a country based on democracy, diversity, and inclusion opened the door for a new understanding of the nation as part of a hemispheric culture. Standing before his grandfather's grave in Kenya, he had a vision of the elder Obama as a young man: "Through force of will, he will create a life out of the scraps of an unknown world, and the memories of a world rendered obsolete."[46]

Words that applied to him, but that also apply to all denizens of the Americas. By living as both Ariel and Caliban, in noble tension with Prospero, on the presidential chair of the hemisphere's signature nation, Obama *showed the way*.

Conclusion

We should offer here our conclusions, based on well-researched observations. And yet we find ourselves, like the Argentinian sage Jorge Luis Borges, having only "time-honored perplexities" to offer.[47] We acknowledge that this story is a brief history of the perplexities of Americans as they have navigated the tempestuous waters of a holy search for cultural identity. It is also an examination of a moment of mythopoetic *anagnorisis* or revelation, prompted by the U.S. presidency of Barack Obama.

The *Account of the Antiquities of the Indians* (1493) by Fray Ramon Pané; the *Royal Commentaries of the Incas* (1609) by the Inca Garcilaso de la Vega; the reports of the shipwreck in the Bermudas of the *Sea Venture*, consulted by Shakespeare in the composition of *The Tempest* (1611); the introductory *loa* [praise] to Sor Juana Inés de la Cruz's *Divine Narcissus* (1690); Jose Hernández's epic *Martin Fierro* and Walt Whitman's mythic appropriation of the American landscape—these were all precursors to the adoption of Shakespeare's Caliban by Latin American political philosophers of the last two centuries to signify a complex, scarcely understood, yet acknowledged American identity.

Before the phenomenon of the assumption of Barack Obama, we as a nation have reacted with perplexity. He is neither black nor white; a Nobel peace prize winner who has waged unremitting war; a politician willing to compromise but who does not hesitate to take executive action. He is a figure unbound—a Caliban who belies Prospero's characterizations. To our own petrified European classifications of the American experience, he replies with the Burkean formula: I am neither, but rather both/and.

Thus, our image of Obama as juggler is not an answer, but rather a hieroglyph containing an undeciphered mystery. Our viewpoint of Obama as Caliban is not an explanation, but rather a heraldic symbol that situates his presidency in a hemispheric context, and that makes him kin to past American political leaders such as Louverture and Benito Juárez.

Obama's Calibanesque self is a mirror reflection of our own self. Whether we like it or not—and regardless of our ethnic origins—we too are African and European, Native and Asian, both Christian and Muslim. As we traverse the alchemy of the cultural heritages that have peopled this continent, we would do well to keep in mind the dictum of African-American Pulitzer prize winner, Charles Gordone: We are different, but we are the same. A paradox that leads to a perplexity, but also a star that beckons a sacred quest.

Notes

1. Material in this chapter was first published as Robert L. Ivie and Oscar Giner, "Barack Obama at the Threshold of a New America," in *Reconsidering Obama: Reflections on Rhetoric*, ed. Robert Terrill (New York: Peter Lang, 2017), 69–87.
2. Robert L. Ivie and Oscar Giner, "More Good, Less Evil: Contesting the Mythos of National Insecurity in the 2008 Presidential Primaries," *Rhetoric & Public Affairs* 121, no. 2 (2009): 279–301; Robert L. Ivie and Oscar Giner, "American Exceptionalism in a Democratic Idiom: Transacting the Mythos of Change in the 2008 Presidential Campaign," *Communication Studies* 60, no. 4 (2009): 359–75.
3. Robert L. Ivie, "Depolarizing the Discourse of American Security: Constitutive Properties of Positive Peace in Barack Obama's Rhetoric of Change," in *Philosophy After Hiroshima*, ed. Edward Demenchonok (Newcastle upon Tyne: Cambridge Scholars Publishing, 2010), 233–61; Robert L. Ivie, "Obama at West Point: A Study in Ambiguity of Purpose," *Rhetoric & Public Affairs* 14, no. 4 (2011): 727–59; Robert L. Ivie and Oscar Giner, *Hunt the Devil: A Demonology of US War Culture* (Tuscaloosa: University of Alabama Press, 2015), 128–30.
4. Jason Gilmore, Penelope Sheets, and Charles Rowling, "Make No Exceptions Save One: American Exceptionalism, the American Presidency, and the Age of Obama," *Communication Monographs* 83, no. 4 (2016): 510.
5. Michael Kazin, *The Populist Persuasion: An American History*, rev. ed. (Ithaca, NY: Cornell University Press, 1998), 292.
6. Ironically, Obama's peace rhetoric established "a moral foundation for future conflicts," according to Joshua Reeves and Matthew S. May, "The Peace Rhetoric of a War President: Barak Obama and the Just War Legacy," *Rhetoric & Public Affairs* 16, no. 4 (2013): 623–50.
7. Dana Milbank, "Barack Obama, the Reluctant Warrior," *Washington Post*, July 6, 2016, https://www.washingtonpost.com/opinions/barack-obama-the-reluctant-warrior/2016/07/06/ac2aacb4-43ba-11e6-88d0-6adee48be8bc_story.html.
8. For a discussion of Obama's rhetorical two-sidedness, see Robert E. Terrill, *Double-Consciousness and the Rhetoric of Barack Obama: The Price and Promise of Citizenship* (Columbia: University of South Carolina Press, 2015).
9. Ivie, "Obama at West Point," 727–59.
10. Robert E. Terrill, "An Uneasy Peace: Barack Obama's Nobel Peace Prize Lecture," *Rhetoric & Public Affairs* 14, no. 4 (2011): 761–79.
11. Ivie, "Depolarizing the Discourse of American Security," 233–61.
12. Ivie and Giner, "More Good, Less Evil," 279–301.
13. Ivie and Giner, "American Exceptionalism in a Democratic Idiom," 359–75.
14. Roger Cohen, "Obama's Implicit Foreign Policy," *New York Times*, February 26, 2016, http://www.nytimes.com/2016/02/26/opinion/obamas-implicit-foreign-policy.html?_r=0.
15. Greg Jaffe, "Which Barack Obama Speech Is the One for the History Books?," *Washington Post*, July 22, 2016, https://www.washingtonpost.com/posteverything/wp/2016/07/22/which-barack-obama-speech-is-the-one-for-the-history-books/.

16 Barack Obama, "Remarks by the President at the 50th Anniversary of the Selma to Montgomery Marches," March 7, 2015, Office of the Press Secretary, The White House, https://www.whitehouse.gov/the-press-office/2015/03/07/remarks-president-50th-anniversary-selma-montgomery-marches.

17 See Matthew Guterl, *American Mediterranean: Southern Slaveholders in the Age of Emancipation* (Cambridge, MA: Harvard University Press, 2008).

18 José Juan Arrom, *Hispanoamérica: Panorama Contemporáneo de Su Cultura* (New York: Harper and Row, 1969), 7; Madison Smart Bell, *Toussaint Louverture* (New York: Pantheon Books, 2007), 7, 20–1.

19 Laurent Dubois and John D. Garrigus, eds., *Slave Revolution in the Caribbean, 1789–1904: A Brief History with Documents* (New York: Palgrave Macmillan, 2006), 128.

20 Hugh Thomas, *Cuba: The Pursuit of Freedom* (New York: Harper and Row, 1971), 77. José Martí (1853–95) was a precursor of Spanish American Modernism and the Apostle of Cuban independence.

21 Madison Smart Bell, *Toussaint Louverture* (New York: Pantheon Books, 2007), 30; Russwurm was the second black college graduate in the U.S. and future co-editor and co-publisher of the first black newspaper, *Freedom's Journal*. See John B. Russwurm, "The Condition and Prospects of Haiti," *The Black Past: Remembered and Reclaimed*, http://www.blackpast.org/1826-john-b-russwurm-condition-and-prospects-haiti; José Martí, "Henry Garnet, Notable Orator Negro," in *Obras Completas* (1882; La Habana: Editorial Nacional de Cuba, 1964), 13:325; Henry Highland Garnet, "An Address to the Slaves of the United States," *The Black Past: Remembered and Reclaimed*, http://www.blackpast.org/1843-henry-highland-garnet-address-slaves-united-states; "Frederick Douglass Speech in Chicago: Lecture on Haiti," http://faculty.webster.edu/corbetre/haiti/history/1844-1915/douglass.htm.

22 William Shakespeare, "The Tempest," in *The Yale Shakespeare*, ed. Wilbur R. Cross and Tucker Brooke (New York: Barnes and Noble, 1993). All references to Shakespeare's plays are from this edition. Text references are to act, scene, and line.

23 Rubén Darío, "El triunfo de Calibán," *El Tiempo*, May 20, 1898, http://www.biblioteca.org.ar/libros/155.pdf; Emir Rodriguez Monegal, "The Metamorphoses of Caliban," http://www.archivodeprensa.edu.uy/biblioteca/emir_rodriguez_monegal/bibliografia/prensa/artpren/diacritics/diacritics_77.htm.

24 Emir Rodríguez Monegal, ed., *The Borzoi Anthology of Latin American Literature* (New York: Alfred A. Knopf, 1977), 1: 371–3, and "The Metamorphoses of Caliban"; José Enrique Rodó, *Ariel*, ed. Gordon Brotherston (Cambridge: Cambridge University Press, 1967), 22, 86, 56, 66, 54–5, 43, 26.

25 Simon Schama, *Rough Crossings: Britain, the Slaves and the American Revolution* (New York: Harper Collins, 2006), 235; Phillis Wheatley, "On Being Brought from Africa to America," http://www.poetryfoundation.org/poems-and-poets/poems/detail/45465; Dion Boucicault, "The Octoroon," in *Early American Drama*, ed. Jeffrey H. Richards (New York: Penguin Books, 1997), 449–94; Alejandro Tapia y Rivera, "La cuarterona," in *Obras Completas* (San Juan, PR: Instituto de Cultura Puertorriqueña, 1968), 2: 671–772. Tapia y Rivera (1826–82) was Puerto Rico's first great playwright.

26 Bertrade Ngo-Ngijol Banoum, "Négritude," *New York Public Library*, http://exhibitions.nypl.org/africanaage/essay-negritude.html#intro; Aimé Césaire, *Notebook of a Return to the Native Land*, trans. Clayton Eshleman and Annette Smith (1939; Middletown, CT: Wesleyan University Press, 2001), 43; Souleymane Bachir Diagne, "Introduction," in *A Season in the Congo*, ed. Aimé Césaire (London: Seagull Books, 2010), vii–xv.
27 Aimé Césaire, *A Tempest*, trans. Richard Miller (New York: Ubu Repertory Theatre Publications, 1992), 6, 65, 67–8; Aimé Césaire, *Une Tempete*, https://is.muni.cz/el/1421/jaro2014/FJI3B777X/tempete.pdf.
28 Brotherston, 2–8; Rodó, 100; Robert Louis Stevenson, *Dr. Jekyll and Mr. Hyde* (1886; New York: Bantam Books, 1985), 80.
29 Fray Ramón Pané, *An Account of the Antiquities of the Indians* (Durham, NC: Duke University Press, 1999), 31n132; Roberto Fernández Retamar, "Caliban," in *Caliban and Other Essays*, trans. Lynn Garafola, David Arthur McMurray, and Roberto Márquez (Minneapolis: University of Minnesota Press, 1989), 6–9.
30 Retamar, 6–9.
31 José Martí, "Our America," in *Selected Writings*, ed. and trans. Esther Allen (New York: Penguin Books, 2002), 293–4; Retamar, 4, 14.
32 Kristine Vanden Berghe, "The Forgotten Caliban of Aníbal Ponce," in *Constellation Caliban: Figurations of a Character*, ed. Nadia Lie and Theo D'haen (Amsterdam: Editions Rodópi, 1997), 187; Aníbal Ponce, "Ariel o la Agonía de una Obstinada Ilusión," *Obras* (La Habana: Casa de las Américas, 1975), 275–92; Darío, "El triunfo de Calibán."
33 Rodó, 91.
34 Retamar, 40.
35 For recorded reactions to Obama's victory on election night, 2008, see https://www.youtube.com/watch?v=X1HSnnDfCks and https://www.youtube.com/watch?v=HMHpib5ZNCc.
36 All references to the Bible are from the Authorized King James Version.
37 Aimé Césaire, *Notebook of a Return to the Native Land*, 44; Barack Obama, *Dreams from My Father: A Story of Race and Inheritance* (1995; New York: Random House Large Print, 2004), 681; "Transcript: 'This is your victory,' says Obama," http://edition.cnn.com/2008/POLITICS/11/04/obama.transcript/; quoted in Jesse Washington, "Obama's True Colors: Black, White… or Neither?" *Los Angeles Daily News*, December 14, 2008, http://www.dailynews.com/20081214/obamas-true-colors-black-white-or-neither.
38 Obama, *Dreams*, 37, 16.
39 Césaire, 43; Retamar, 45.
40 Obama, *Dreams*, 125, 169.
41 "Transcript: Barack Obama's Speech on Race," March 18, 2008, http://www.npr.org/templates/story/story.php?storyId=88478467. For a discussion of the mythos of Obama's appeal to the American dream, see Robert C. Rowland and John M. Jones, "One Dream: Barack Obama, Race, and the American Dream," *Rhetoric & Public Affairs* 14, no. 1 (2011): 125–54. See also Susanna Dilliplane, "Race, Rhetoric, and Running for President: Unpacking the Significance of Barack Obama's 'A More Perfect Union' Speech," *Rhetoric & Public Affairs* 15, no. 1 (2012): 127–52.
42 Quoted in Bell, 201, 205.

43 This notion achieved the zenith of popularity in our modern age: a Facebook page and several *YouTube videos*. See https://www.facebook.com/204795082996380/posts/555983584544193; and https://www.youtube.com/watch?v=-i-7dm4Kgkk; also "President Obama the Antichrist? Not really, but he's 'paving the way,' evangelists say," http://www.christiantoday.com/article/president.obama.the.antichrist.not.really.but.hes.paving.the.way.evangelists.say/61548.htm. The racist themes of Birther rhetoric are discussed by Vincent M. Pham, "Our Foreign President Barack Obama: The Racial Logic of Birther Discourses," *Journal of International and Intercultural Communication* 8, no. 2 (2015): 86–107.

44 Obama, *Dreams from My Father*, 161; "Remarks by the President at Memorial Service for Fallen Dallas Police Officers," https://www.whitehouse.gov/the-press-office/2016/07/12/remarks-president-memorial-service-fallen-dallas-police-officers.

45 Eugene Robinson, "Obama Has Helped Us Peer into the Racial Divide," *The Washington Post*, July 4, 2016, https://www.washingtonpost.com/opinions/obama-has-helped-us-peer-into-the-racial-divide/2016/07/14/5794b840-49f3-11e6-90a8-fb84201e0645_story.html.

46 Obama, *Dreams from My Father*, 650.

47 Jorge Luis Borges, *This Craft of Verse* (Cambridge: Harvard University Press, 2000), 2.

· 2 ·

INCANTATIONS OF EMPIRE[1]

Empire is a landscape of petrified metaphors in which dreams of greatness come to rest in a soldier's grave. Its capital city is a wasteland of illusions that do not fade. The young and the old walk the streets without clear purpose or star. Guided by the logic of realism, a crowd of living corpses greets the passage of a knight's skeleton, encased in armor, riding a chestnut warhorse. Citizens cheer even after losing all their children to the business of war. A bishop with staff and miter bows his head in adoration of old gods. The prophet is slain in the monk's cold cell. Ancient, venerable buildings are covered with thorns and brambles. As the prophet warned, they have become a court for owls and a residence for dragons.

Such is the fated discourse of empire, viewed symbolically from a mythic standpoint. It is a discourse that encompasses the fixed image of a death struggle between civilization and savagery sustained by the mythic incantations of rhetorical rituals that naturalize an attitude of war. Like any orthodoxy, empire overreaches when closed off to critique. The ruling order is rendered insensible, unresponsive, and ultimately vulnerable to the dynamic forces of pluralism and self-determination.

Imperial Orthodoxy

Empire is a woolly concept for a manifold condition of political, economic, cultural, and military hegemony. It designates a preponderance of power, a degree of influence and authority comprising a state of domination expressed as a hierarchy of relations. It represents itself in reified images as the natural order of things. Its reigning symbols are figures of speech made so routine and conventional by everyday use that they sound flat, appear literal, turn rigid, and lose their symbolic resonance. Empire, by this reckoning, is the rule of politically enervated imagery, a regime of gestures no longer vital or flexible enough to adapt to a dynamic world. It is an order maintained by violence.

In view of the global militarization that both preceded and followed World War II, George Orwell warned that a debased language produced a "reduced state of consciousness," which was "favorable to political conformity." Three years before the publication of *1984*, he wrote: "Orthodoxy, of whatever color, seems to demand a lifeless, imitative style."[2]

Friedrich Nietzsche captured the essence of metaphors-reduced-to-reified-concepts when he defined truth as "a movable host of metaphors, metonymies, and anthropomorphisms: in short, a sum of human relations which have been poetically and rhetorically intensified, transferred, and embellished, and which, after long usage, seem to a people to be fixed, canonical, and binding." So-called truths, he observed, "are metaphors that have become worn out and have been drained of sensuous force." Concepts, and the logics they entail, are the "*residue of a metaphor.*"[3]

Imperial nations are prone to literalizing metaphors into truths. Vico's *New Science*, contra Descartes, understood the cycle of cultural innovation and decline as a process of insight followed by development leading to decay.[4] Metaphor, in Vico's model, is the linguistic vehicle of *ingenium*, the human faculty for seeing similarities among differences. As a creative act of knowledge, an exercise of imagination, it produces fresh insights. As a rhetorical act, it finds and draws on images that function as *topoi* to invent arguments and build logics into socio-cultural constructs that resist critique and demand conformity in the name of truth. Society rigidifies and crumbles as it loses touch with its mythic origins. It fails to recognize that its concepts were founded on dynamic metaphors, themselves myths in miniature, visions that evoke narratives.

Understanding society as a cyclical process of symbolic action brings into focus the relationship of rhetoric and reality to myth and ritual. Kenneth

Burke provocatively explains how rhetoric cycles through the victimage ritual to sustain hierarchies by sacrificing scapegoats. The governing order is ritually redeemed "by blaming all its many troubles on the other." Hence, the imperial "Cult of the Kill."[5] In the nineteenth century, José Martí warned that no empire is innocent of what Burke later called the "exaltation" of sacrificial human offerings:

> [Among American Indians] there are sacrifices of beautiful young maidens made to invisible gods in Heaven just as in Greece, where often there were so many sacrifices that there was no need to build altars for new ceremonies, because the pile of ashes of the last burn was so high that the priests could lay their sacrificial victims on them; there were human sacrifices like the one by Abraham the Hebrew, who tied Isaac over the wood pile to kill him with his own hands because he thought he heard voices from Heaven which ordered him to plunge his knife into his son, so that his blood would satiate his god; there were public sacrifices in the Plaza Mayor in Spain, in front of bishops and kings, when the Inquisition burned men alive, with pomp and circumstance, while the Madrid ladies observed the burning from their balconies. Ignorance and superstition turn human beings into barbarians in all nations. And about the Indians more than is just has been said about these things by the victorious Spaniards, who exaggerated and invented the defects of the defeated race, so that their own cruelty would appear just and convenient to the world.[6]

Mark Twain once lamented that a handful of Missouri lynchers had "given us a character and labeled us with a name," making the U.S. known globally as the "United States of Lyncherdom."[7]

Empire's Resistance to Critique

Comic correctives, in Kenneth Burke's sense of the term, are required to deflect the tragic trajectory of victimage, to bridge the human divide, and to reduce the imperial impulse to dominate and kill.[8] Empire is devoid of a comic perspective. Acknowledging and retrieving dead metaphors would be destabilizing. Instead, the cultural and political legitimacy of American empire rests precariously on a lifeless image of democracy. It exists in a state of symbolic denial. All that remains of democracy in the imperial image is an empty gesture, a simulacrum, a trace of collective self-governance, a flicker of equality and inclusion.

In 1922, H.L. Mencken asked himself the question "Why am I still here?" after American artists and intellectuals had departed—and called others to depart—U.S. shores for "fairer lands" in Europe. Mencken's essay, "On Being an American," stands as an engaging critique of American exceptionalism:

> Here, more than anywhere else that I know of or have heard of, the daily panorama of human existence, of private and communal folly—the unending procession of governmental extortions and chicaneries, of commercial brigandages and throat-slittings, of theological buffooneries, of aesthetic ribaldries, of legal swindles and harlotries, of miscellaneous rogueries, villainies, imbecilities, grotesqueries, and extravagances—is so inordinately gross and preposterous, so perfectly brought up to the highest conceivable amperage, so steadily enriched with an almost fabulous daring and originality, that only the man who was born with a petrified diaphragm can fail to laugh himself to sleep every night, and to awake every morning with all the eager, unflagging expectation of a Sunday-school superintendent touring the Paris peep shows.

A century later, one might conclude that the glaring flaws of the nation's political system are not a particular idiosyncrasy, but rather a central element of North American culture. "Here in the very citadel of democracy," Mencken wrote, "we found and cherish a clown *dynasty!*"⁹

Mencken's characterization is the product of the vision of a trickster prophet. Like Babylon, the Republic has "glorified herself," and her citizens—plagued by the worms of belief in a manifest destiny—have become biblical scribes and Pharisees: "whited sepulchers," beautiful outside, but "within full of dead men's bones, and of all uncleanness."[10] In the entrails of empire, overrun by the weight of dead metaphors, trickster's howl is not heard and trickster's humor is ignored. Prophets are killed, scourged, or crucified only when they threaten empires.

Imperial rule is lethal, but it is also rhetorically moribund. A worn regime of exclusion, surveillance, and coercion displaces the spirited politics of inclusion and contestation. Canonical images operate in the war state below the threshold of critical reflection. They goad the public to defend the citadel of democracy and to smite projected demons. The act of demonizing adversaries denatures peacemaking and naturalizes warfare. Depicting war as rhythmical, timeless, migratory, clean, and heroic lends it a sense of necessity and inevitability. A vast landscape of habituated imagery diminishes political life, reduces political discourse to the mythic incantations of war propaganda, and renders polity robotic like drone warfare.

The Roman Empire has served as a constant model for the imperial aspirations of a young U.S. nation, complete with restrained but unresolved tensions between the quest for greatness and a call for justice. The story of Spartacus, "founded on that passage of Roman history where the slaves—Gallic, Spanish,

Thracian and African—rose against their masters, and formed themselves into a military organization," proved meaningful to the American cultural imaginary in the nineteenth century. The first American-born tragedian Edwin Forrest (1806–72) won national renown in the role of Spartacus in Robert Montgomery Bird's (1806–54) *The Gladiator*. Walt Whitman witnessed a performance of the play in 1846: "From footlights to lobby doors—from floor to dome—were packed crowds of people last night at the Park Theatre, New York, to see Mr. Forrest in *The Gladiator*." Whitman admired Forrest's delivery of the speech of Spartacus "in which he attributes the grandeur and the wealth of Rome, to her devastation of other countries."[11] In chains, Spartacus speaks when he sees the palaces of Rome for the first time:

> If Romans had not been fiends, Rome had never been great! Whence came this greatness, but from the miseries of subjugated nations? How many myriads of happy people ... were slain like beasts of the field, that Rome might fatten upon their blood, and become great? ... There is not a palace upon these hills that cost not the lives of a thousand innocent men; there is no deed of greatness ye can boast, but it was achieved upon the ruin of a nation; there is no joy you can feel, but its ingredients are blood and tears.[12]

In 1960, just before the John F. Kennedy administration assumed power heralding a "New Frontier," Stanley Kubrick's film *Spartacus* premiered in Hollywood. The screenplay was written by Dalton Trumbo, based on the novel by Howard Fast.[13] Both writers had been imprisoned and blacklisted in Hollywood during the national persecution of film artists and producers with past communist associations. In the film (produced by Kirk Douglas' Bryna Productions), the Roman patrician Crassus (Laurence Olivier) shows his young slave Antoninus (Tony Curtis) a panoramic view of Rome from his villa. Roman cohorts march in the distance *en route* to quell Spartacus' slave rebellion. Crassus describes the fabled city in the distance, and the empire for which it stands:

> The might, the majesty, the terror of Rome. ... There is the power that bestrides the known world, like a colossus. No nation can withstand Rome. No man can withstand her. ... You must serve her. You must abase yourself before her. You must grovel at her feet. You must love her.

The American Legion sent a letter to "17,000 local posts" warning them to NOT SEE *Spartacus*. One influential columnist wrote: "The story was sold ... from a book written by a Commie and the screen script was written by a

Commie, so don't go see it." But JFK—with a more perceptive understanding of mythic evocations—"sneaked out of the White House in the middle of a snowstorm one night, to go see *Spartacus* at the Warner Theater."[14] The American public followed the lead of its young president.

Transgressive Tricksters

Living in the post-9/11 war state is a stupefying experience akin to the "psychic numbing" of Cold War nuclearism and the prospect of mutual assured destruction.[15] War delineates the arc of U.S. history and permeates the whole of American culture.[16] Militarism is as unexceptional and unremarkable as the air one breathes. It is an everyday occurrence and a totalizing worldview fully integrated with the nation's favorite modes of entertainment.[17] Indeed, as Patrick Deer notes, militarization has blurred wartime and daily life in U.S. culture, politics, and society, which marks the standing relationship between empire and war culture that normalizes a permanent state of warfare in the name of assuring freedom and deterring aggressors while "silencing, compartmentalizing, and excluding dissenting perspectives."[18]

War culture is the foundation of politics, the defining feature of society, and the operative discourse for the normalization of violence at home and abroad.[19] Even the primal myth of American exceptionalism, with its notions of national innocence and superiority, is reified in public discourse. The religious image of redemptive warfare by a righteous people on an errand to vanquish evil and to spread the blessings of liberty is a taken-for-granted premise of secular society.[20] The pursuit of peace, as cultural critic Jon Simons observes, is the liberal state's justification for war.[21] U.S. militarism operates rhetorically in denial of its imperialism.[22]

On posters during a presidential trip in 2002, on car bumper stickers, on signs raised by protesters in Washington during the second inaugural, the harsh, mocking laughter of trickster was heard ridiculing George W. Bush: "Send the twins to Iraq!" The call was for the president to send his 20-year-old daughters to serve in his war. It pointed out the hypocrisy of North American ruling classes and conjured the political lessons contained in the classic tale of the Greek armies that mustered at Aulis for the Trojan War.

Send the twins to Iraq because the Achaeans have gathered at Aulis and profaned the countryside, killing a hare "bursting with young unborn," and Artemis "the undefiled" has bound the fleet with crosswinds unless Iphigeneia is slaughtered by her own father. In spite of its seeming barbarity, the command of the virgin goddess of nature and wild things was a metaphor for a wise policy that imposed trauma in order to arrest war. Before the Greeks sailed to Ilion, the allied host was forced to prove its conviction that the war was worthy and necessary.[23]

An exchange between King Agamemnon and Queen Clytemnestra in Euripides' *Iphigeneia at Aulis* reveals the political conflict that could be solved only through Iphigeneia's execution. The Queen, protecting her daughter, argues:

> Let Menelaos
> to whom it matters most, after all, cut his own
> daughter's throat.

Agamemnon, affirming the political necessity of Greek nation-states, replies:

> Being Greeks,
> we must not be subject to barbarians,
> we must not let them carry off our wives.

Proof of his conviction will be the sacrifice of his firstborn daughter, for Artemis demands a human tax before the war is fought.[24]

There is no guarantee that trickster's twists and turns will yield a comic corrective, for war making as an expression of personal and national identity is easy relative to peace building. The "rhetorical presumption of war's necessity makes the violence regrettable but [seemingly] sane, rational, right, proper, and easier than bearing the heavy burden of dissenting from war"; "placing one's self or loved ones in harm's way seems less difficult and more reassuring than questioning the necessity, legitimacy, or sanity of war in any given case."[25] This is the tyranny of war culture, but trickster's opportunity turns up most readily when the warmonger is extracted a cost or made to pay a personal price for his war.

In Euripides' *Iphigeneia in Tauris*, the daughter of Agamemnon is spirited away by Artemis at the moment of death and taken to the land of the Taurians. Embittered at the grave injustices committed against her, Iphigeneia becomes the priestess who dedicates human victims at the sacrificial shrine of Artemis. Only when it comes to sacrificing her brother Orestes does she acknowledge her complicity in the human sacrifices of the Taurians. Only when the sacrificial knife threatens our own do we feel dissonance and recognize our own shadow projections for what they are. The emotional distress produced by trauma, especially when the trauma is brought home to those in positions of power, conjures trickster as compensation, in an attempt to restore harmony and balance to the universe. The resolution of Iphigeneia's tension through a tricksterish recognition of her victim as her own brother—a comic corrective to the tragic plot—allows her to reject the sacrificial knife and escape to Argos with Orestes, with the blessings of Athena.

Empire's Continuous War on Evil

The basic logic of U.S. war culture is premised unreflectively on an illusory specter of chaos. To regress into chaos is to reenter a dark, formless, and meaningless void. Chaos symbolizes disorder, a condition of disorientation, a negation of life. Evildoers, appeasement, dominoes, and containment are metaphors taken literally in the context of U.S. foreign affairs. They convey the fear of a cataclysmic event, a collapse of civilization, which prods the nation to preserve a tenuous world order. In columnist Charles Krauthammer's opinion, "The alternative to U.S. leadership is either global chaos or dominance by the likes of China, Russia and Iran."[26] Likewise, intones the U.S. Department of State, terrorism is the scourge of world order, a menace that can be removed only by prolonged warfare:

> Terrorist networks currently pose the greatest national security threat to the United States. ... [Al-Qaida] aims to overthrow the existing world order and replace it with a reactionary, authoritarian, transnational entity. This threat will be sustained over a protracted period (decades not years) and will require a global response.[27]

This logic makes a perfect enemy of the Islamic State. The barbarity of the designated enemy affirms America's heroic role as enlightened defender of civilization. The American president considers what kind and how much of a military engagement the U.S. should undertake against the "cancer" of the Islamic State in Iraq and Syria. High-ranking officials in the administration (the Chairman of the Joint Chiefs of Staff, the Secretary of Defense, and the Secretary of State) characterize the Islamic State as a "barbaric" and "apocalyptic" terrorist organization that must be "contained," "defeated," and "destroyed" because it poses an "imminent threat." This enemy is "beyond anything we've seen," the Defense Secretary insists, "so we must prepare for everything."[28]

Richard Cohen, a political commentator who supported the George W. Bush administration's decision to invade Iraq, insists that the U.S. is "once again up against the question of evil." The Islamic State is "pure evil." It "murders with abandon. It seems to love death the way the fascists once did." This reincarnation of the Nazis, Cohen asserts, is "beyond explication." It would be "futile and tasteless" to lay the blame on the U.S., colonialists of old, Zionists of today, or the rich and powerful. No one can understand a Hitler. Any attempt to explain the inexplicable amounts to a justification of "evil returned, evil that can be understood only as beyond understanding." The "category of evil remains useful" because "it assigns agency where it belongs." Evil simply "needs to be eliminated."[29]

This stark reification of evil proscribes any attempt to understand the causes, motives, and reasons behind the violence and thereby exonerates the U.S. for past, present, and future actions in the Middle East. It stuns a people's mental faculties, blinds them to the complexity of the situation, and commits the nation to a narrow mindset of eradication as the only viable option, while exposing would-be critics to the charge of condoning atrocity.

Imperial warfare is continuous and self-perpetuating. It possesses a certain rhythm, an ebb and flow of featured enemies, as it shifts from venue to venue. With the emergence of the Islamic State, Abu Bakr al-Baghdadi is declared the world's most powerful, violent, and anti-American jihadist, Osama bin Laden's true heir. Middle Eastern chaos and extremism are deemed resurgent.[30] The rhythm of enemy-making ritualistically renews war, keeping the public synchronized with the war state and resigned to the global war of terrorism, while rendering its consequences psychologically remote. Its modality is "light war," observes Jessy Ohl, which "places few demands on thought, feeling, and attention."[31]

The rhythm of imperial warfare is as constant as the ocean tides. The symbol of the sea, as Michael Osborn has explained, is archetypal.[32] It sets off a primal emotional response. It can convey a sense of inevitability, peril, adventure, and redemption. At the turn of the twentieth century, U.S. Senator Albert Beveridge imagined the ocean as an avenue of U.S. imperialism that rendered the world contiguous. In a speech at the Naval War College, Theodore Roosevelt recalled the "glorious triumphs at sea" of the War of 1812. Before "everyman of really far-sighted patriotism," he argued for the "possession of a sufficient" armed navy fleet:

> Those who wish to see this country at peace with foreign nations will be wise if they place reliance upon a first-class fleet of first-class battleships rather than on any arbitration treaty which the wit of man can devise. ... Peace is a goddess only when she comes with sword girt on thigh. The ship of state can be steered safely only when it is possible to bring her against any fore with "her leashed thunders gathering for the leap."[33]

The continuous ebb and flow of the global war on terrorism is a naturalizing balm. It gives imperial warfare a comprehensible form. The tide of war rises and falls rhythmically with the pull of the moon. One day, the news is military success against the Islamic State.[34] The enemy's advance has been halted; plans are afoot to retake the lost territories. High tide. The next day, the news is military setback: "The main al-Qaeda affiliate in Syria is extending its control over a swath of territory that was until recently held by the collapsing moderate opposition, jeopardizing U.S. plans to form a new rebel force to fight extremists."[35] Low tide.

Dead metaphors impart to imperial warfare a sense of timelessness. The mythos of timelessness goes unnoticed as it makes war an ongoing, continual, unending struggle against relentless evil, an eternal cycle of attack-defense-victory-attack, a millennial contest with the devil that transforms chronic conflicts into a transcendent, forever war.

Speaking at the National Defense University, President Obama allowed that America was at a "crossroads" where it must define its effort "not as a boundless 'global war on terror,' but rather as a series of persistent, targeted efforts to dismantle specific networks of violent extremists."[36] The language of "a series" represents war as persistent. Continuity intersects with change at a point of transition. Invisible Hecate, goddess of the crossroads, mythically inhabits this ghostly place where dark deeds congress with her beauty and purity, her timeless presence suggesting the uncertainty that flows from the coincidence of good and evil. The symbol and image of Hecate is undetectable in a presidential speech the through-line of which begins with the acknowledgment that Americans are deeply ambivalent about the war. So was Macbeth after hearing the triple prophecy of the witches upon Hecate's heath. The cautionary words of Banquo fall on deaf ears:

> Oftentimes, to win us to our harm
> The instruments of darkness tell us truths,
> Win us with honest trifles, to betray's
> In deepest consequence.[37]

The present war, like every war, intoned Obama, must "come to an end"; yet, "our systematic effort to dismantle terrorist organizations must continue" because "our nation is still threatened by terrorists." America's fight enters "a new phase." The U.S. cannot remain on a "perpetual wartime footing," but it must "continue to fight terrorism." Success on all fronts requires a "long-term strategy" and "sustained engagement."[38] War persists and will continue, like the line of Banquo's heirs, "to th' crack of doom."[39]

Migratory-Pristine-Heroic-Routine War

War is forever, and it migrates. It moves from one place to another in search of enemies to engage. Obama's speech was about defending the homeland by pursuing terrorists in distant lands. The long war against terrorism began with 9/11, sending Americans first to Afghanistan and Iraq, then the battleground shifted to Yemen, Somalia, and North Africa. The continuing hunt for al Qaeda affiliates takes U.S. military forces to "distant and unforgiving places ... remote tribal regions ... caves and walled compounds ... empty deserts and rugged mountains." These are the faraway places that constitute the "imminent threat" to "our cities at home and our facilities abroad."[40] History advises America to pursue terrorist leaders and organizations relentlessly. The President's image of place does not imply everywhere war so much as migratory war, something that travels, that is mobile and peripatetic, that perpetually moves from one battlefield to the next. The U.S. follows the threat wherever the enemy appears.

Imperial war is also technologically clean. Drones—unmanned aerial vehicles—are a signature weapon of clean, precisely targeted, warfare. In the insect world, drones are fast flying male bees with big eyes but no stinger. In the military world, drones are equipped with advanced optics and armed with Hellfire missiles. They are named Predator and Reaper and used to smite evil terrorists. The mythical undertone of these slayer drones with their Gorgon Stare is underappreciated for its power to legitimize automated warfare. The lethal Reaper drone insinuates the Grim Reaper, death's personification in the figure of the hooded skeleton carrying a scythe to sever body from soul. Just as the biblical Angel of Death, the Reaper drone serves as imperial America's destroying angel.

Clean war is the work of the gods. Its contrast with dirty war is ritually purifying, even if the perpetrators are the empire's own warriors. The

Oscar-nominated documentary, *Dirty Wars*, is illustrative.[41] The war crimes of Commander-in-Chief Barack Obama and his Joint Special Operations Command (JSOC) are uncovered and exposed for public condemnation. The film, featuring the investigative journalism of Jeremy Scahill, unfolds in the style of a conspiracy thriller. JSOC is a "shadowy outfit" with a growing "hit list" and a presidential order to kill. These special forces are "assassins" killing innocent civilians in the night, "war masters" fighting a war of terror, which extends from home invasions to torture and murder. They make America look like a terror state, until they kill Osama bin Laden to earn official recognition and public acclaim.

Condemning dirty wars indirectly affirms wars that conform to the rules. Rule-governed war is just war. War itself is obliquely redeemed by the negative examples of rogue soldiers (and the war crimes of enemies). Purifying rituals put the nation in touch with the divine. They serve as an unacknowledged mythic "control system" for glorifying militarism.[42]

America's pristine-migratory-perpetual warfare is heroic, the pride of patriots. Soldiers fighting evil terrorists are empire's equivalent to the biblical David slaying Goliath. In Abrahamic mythology, God enabled His people to destroy evil giants and to occupy their land. The chosen people ousted outsized pagans from the Promised Land. Not timid Saul, but brave David, "a man of valor, a warrior," led the army that secured Israel and Judah.[43] Virtue and courage overcome the bluster of evil. The faithful underdog is victorious over those who have "defied the armies of the living God."[44] Imperialism is transformed from aggressor to defender.

The mythic underdog is expected to lose. He is the good guy, not the imperialist with the biggest military budget and the most sophisticated weapons. The expected winner is the foreign giant, the personification of evil savagery. Justice prevails when the little guy surprisingly beats the big guy. Walter Pincus' (*Washington Post*, September 29, 2014) story of the "Islamic State's Bloody Message Machine" is a case in point. The Islamic State, he reports, is a barbaric enemy, but it has developed a twenty-first century global media platform that gives it superpowers. Its propaganda spews forth in social media, pamphlets, magazines, billboards, t-shirts, and baseball caps. The message machine includes professionally staged videos of beheadings and a captive British journalist criticizing the U.S. bombing campaign. Video games are used to recruit more jihadists. "The Islamic State PR team has a big advantage when it comes to the propaganda war" in a region of the world that is "hospitable to anti-West and particularly anti-U.S. messaging." These slick barbarians get away with calling the U.S. president a "mule of the Jews." Americans "will pay the price," they taunt, for meddling with Islam. The U.S. has been out maneuvered on foreign terrain. It must rely on unreliable Iraqis and Syrians to win not only the ground war but also the propaganda war.[45]

Stories like the one Walter Pincus tells tacitly convert the enemy into the giant and assign the U.S. the role of heroic underdog, which helps to sustain an incessant war of terror by a nation that routinely celebrates military heroes. The hero, one of mythology's central motifs, affirms the national identity by associating it with the courageous warrior, crusader, and rescuer. It tells Americans they are a brave and honorable people, morally inspired, on a quest to overcome evil in the far reaches of the world. It is a primitive story based on a primordial image, an unprocessed attitude about violence and right behavior, Carl Jung observed.[46] The hero fights the forces of darkness. To slay the menacing dragon of evil is to redeem the vulnerable virtues of life.[47]

All of this and more is the naturalized symbol system that imparts automatic and undemocratic consent to imperial war. It makes war justification efficient. It takes the president only 15 ceremonial minutes on primetime television to renew the nation's war commitment by announcing that America's new enemy in the ongoing war on terrorism is the Islamic State. This enemy is neither Islamic nor a state, he says, but instead a terrorist organization that kills innocent people.

The president's speech wastes no time. He steps up to the White House lectern and begins without preliminaries or pause. He reiterates the standard rationale for war: the enemy is "evil"; "it has no vision other than the slaughter of all who stand in its way"; its "acts of barbarism" include killing children, raping and enslaving women, threatening a religious minority with genocide, and beheading two American journalists; the U.S. and its "broad coalition of partners" will meet this threat "with strength and resolve"; America's objective is to "hunt down," "degrade, and ultimately destroy" these terrorists "wherever they are; this is a "steady, relentless" fight for freedom and security and to defend the nation's values; "it will take time to eradicate a cancer like ISIL" [the Islamic State]; but Americans can be confident about the country's future; "American leadership is the one constant in an uncertain world"; "God bless our troops, and may God bless the United States of America." That said, the president turns and walks deliberately away from the lectern. No questions are asked. The president is exercising his authority. He welcomes Congressional support, but it is unnecessary.[48]

If there had been a debate worthy of democracy, questions at issue would have included: Is there a military solution to this problem? What would a political solution to the crisis require? What are the alternatives to military force, including diplomacy and cutting off the flow of weapons and funds to ISIL? Is the retraining of the Iraqi military by the U.S. more likely to be successful than the failed initial training of the Iraqi military by the U.S.? Will today's military commitment eventually grow to include substantial numbers of U.S. combat troops, not just air strikes? How much money will the fight against ISIL require? Is U.S. military intervention counterproductive? Will it serve primarily to recruit more jihadists? What are the chances of the conflict spreading beyond Iraq and Syria? Is there an endpoint, a way out, a measure of victory in a war against ISIL? How enduring is public support for such a war?

Such questions are considered beyond the pale of public discourse in the war state. They are unreasonable, rude, unpatriotic, or simply naïve. War is fact. Information rules the modern world of empire. Objectivity is the standard of thought. Realists think in metrics. All they need is objective data. Facts reflect reality. The war on terror is about defeating an actual enemy. Terrorism is fact. Peacemaking is myth. Myth is primitive, wishful thinking that is neither mathematical nor objective. By this logic, those who dissent from the endless and boundless war on terror are automatically removed to the margins of rationality. Those who support the war, even fervently, are realists.

A kind of secular demonolatry gives to imperial warfare and its supporters the presumption of realism. Russian President Vladimir Putin, the Islamic State, Al-Qaeda, and other demons are the nation's preoccupation, the monsters and fiends sacrificed in war's ongoing victimage ritual. For those who literalize the Bible in a land that sees itself blessed by God, the obsession with salvation from evil spirits promotes conformity, authoritarianism, and an expectation of apocalypse. They are subconsciously massaged by metaphor, symbolism, imagery, and emotionalism, which short-circuits their capacity for critical thinking.[49] This kind of unacknowledged demonology is a secular, not just a fundamentalist and religious, phenomenon in the world of American exceptionalism.

Apocalypse

A continuous, routinized, archetypal war on evil eventually culminates in an apocalyptic discourse of oblivion. It follows the Aristotelian principle of entelechy, borrowed by Kenneth Burke to explain the tragic trajectory of human symbolic action in search of redemption by the slaying of a perfect villain.[50] Imperialistic language goads its adherents to the actualization of its mythic climax in the conquering of an evil enemy. Thus, the ground is prepared for the eruption of Donald Trump.[51]

Trump's unexpected election to the presidency is retrospectively true to form. The mythos of a war culture of a self-proclaimed exceptional nation culminates in the obliteration of evil. Trump would make the nation whole again by expunging that which is foreign and impure. He would return the nation to its "exceptional roots."[52] His rhetoric, as Mary Stuckey observes, is exclusive and violent in ways that bode ill for democratic polity. Its excess of hyperbole, incivility, and nostalgia short-circuit the rationality of self-rule and republican governance.[53] Its use of "weaponized communication tactics to gain compliance and avoid accountability," Jennifer Mercieca argues, renders it dangerous as a source of democratic erosion.[54] Robert Terrill adds that Trump's recursive rhetoric narrows perspective to reinforce existing ideological formations and calcify prejudices. It is a perversely unethical discourse that invites no deliberation—a chaotic concoction of fear, distrust, and triumphalism that is "corrosive to democratic ideals."[55]

The significance of Trump's demagoguery is discernable in its brutishness, which conveys an unwitting prophecy of imperial ruin. Redeeming empire requires demolishing democratic polity. A demagogic misdirection of public discontent sustains an exposed system of economic privilege. In Alison Hearn's terms, the hustle is a symptom of, and alibi for, a "failing political economic system marked by perpetual crisis, where traditional jobs are disappearing and employment is ever more precarious."[56] The violent imagery of Trump's coarse, indecorous, and unapologetic rhetoric, Bonnie Dow argues, feeds a collective fantasy that he will get things done by shaking up politics as usual.[57] In adopting the persona of the populist, the demagogue sacrifices democracy to preserve the hegemony of corporate capitalism.[58]

Trump's authoritarianism would consolidate power over the people. Mark Andrejevic notes Trump's demagogic "jouissance," which provides a kind of pleasure in spectacle that merges entertainment with politics, skepticism with fantasy, and violence with authoritarian tendencies.[59] This is a demagoguery that inclines toward the imperial. It infantilizes the public and fortifies a militant mindset.

Trump's promise of national salvation is a discourse of redemption by demolition. It prompts followers to emote—to express uninhibited feelings of fear, anger, and hatred. It is a seductive spectacle of the wrecking ball well adapted to a media culture of fast-paced, combative entertainment.[60] As envisioned by Trump's chief political strategist, it deconstructs the administrative state.[61] The mythic appeal of the Trumpian "explosion," Kendall Phillips observes, resonates with an affective shift over the preceding decade among many Americans coming to see the government "as a dangerous enemy needing destruction." Popular film at this critical moment, especially in the xenophobic war genre, depicts the government as uncaring and untrustworthy, unwilling or unable to protect white citizens from enemies of color. The narrative of the corrupt state entails the rejection and destruction of the state apparatus itself.[62]

Trump vows to restore lost glory by demolishing non-defense agencies, increasing annual military spending, cutting taxes, dismantling regulations on Wall Street, repealing Obamacare, shredding trade agreements, eliminating government regulations, canceling Obama's executive orders, staying unwanted immigration, and eradicating radical Islamic terrorism. He promises a swift, simple, and emotionally satisfying renovation of a system rigged against the American people. He plays to a fantasy of bootstrapping individualism and unfettered capitalism. He dominates the public agenda in a mercurial display of political clownery and racist innuendo, demonizing opponents without regard for consistency or truth.

Trumpism is raw diversion. Its trope of demolition is cathectic. Brian Ott observes that Trump's tweets are homologous with his speaking style in their simplicity, impulsivity, and incivility.[63] The rawness is visceral and verbal. Message and manner converge. One can sense the rhythmic swing of the sledgehammer in Trump's speech and tweets.

Trump regales his followers with the promise to raze the establishment of political elites in Washington:

> It's happening. It's happening. It's happening.
> ... we inherited a mess. It's a mess.
> ... really terrible trade deals. Horrible trade deals. .... Not going to happen anymore.
> ... we will stop radical Islamic terrorism. We will stop it. Not going to let it happen. Not here. Not going to let it happen.
> ... This is our long-awaited chance to finally get rid of Obamacare. It's a long-awaited chance. We're going to do it. We're going to do it.[64]

And again, Trump speaks in demolition terms of "great, great battles to come," of "eradicating" criminal gangs, withdrawing the U.S. from "the horrible, disastrous, would have been another NAFTA but worse, Trans-Pacific Partnership," having "cleared the way" for the Keystone pipeline, having "scrapped" federal regulations, and doing still more "to drain the swamp."[65]

The belligerent inflection of Trump's rally speech is palpably vicious. He pauses dramatically to watch a protester being removed: "That's right, get him out of here, get him out." The thread of militancy, stitched throughout his speech, links military, police, and border patrol into a single motif of personal safety and homeland security achieved by building a border wall and deporting "illegals." He speaks of visiting with parents of children "viciously killed, violently killed by illegal immigrants." He promises, emphasizing each word, that "<u>we will protect American lives; your family members will not have died in vain</u>." He speaks in the language of war, a war to stop crime that Democrats refuse to fight. Democrats "don't mind drugs pouring in. They don't mind, excuse me, MS-13 coming in." He assures his enthusiastic listeners that he will "keep radical Islamic terrorists the hell out of our country." He reads a poem about a venomous snake that strikes the kind woman who gave it shelter and then mocks her, saying, "You knew damned well I was a snake before you took me in."[66]

The militant tone of Trump's rally rhetoric resonates with the dark demeanor of his inaugural address. The inaugural's haunting image of "American carnage" consists of "rusted out factories scattered like tombstones," an infrastructure that has "fallen into disrepair and decay," "millions upon millions of American workers left behind," and an impoverished country robbed of its unrealized potential by gangs and drugs. He speaks on behalf of a "righteous public," the "forgotten men and women," for whom he will govern with a new purpose and vision. "I will fight for you with every breath of my body." He vows to "unite the civilized world against Radical Islamic Terrorism," which he "will eradicate completely from the face of the earth."[67] Thus, Trump's dark inaugural address echoes his militant campaign theme that "You got to knock the hell out of them. Boom! Boom! Boom!"[68]

The rawness of Trump's demolition trope infuses his rhetoric with a militancy that sustains U.S. militarism under an America First moniker. It represents itself as a discourse of change but maintains status-quo militarism. It is a vehicle of continuity represented as a break from the role of world policeman. "Our military will be given the resources its brave warriors so richly deserve." To keep America safe, the military will get "one of the largest increases in national defense spending in American history" so that they might fight and win wars. His Department of Defense is directed "to develop a plan to demolish and destroy ISIS—a network of lawless savages."[69]

Demolition is Trump's rhetorical hammer. Cataclysm is the political entailment of demolition. Viewing Trump's discourse from the perspective of political myth, as a vehicle of unwitting prophecy, helps to make sense of a perplexing and unsettling spectacle. Prophesy favors symbolism over transparency. Its message is sufficiently vague and ambiguous to require a full measure of interpretation, which allows for multiple and divergent readings. One might discern in Trump's demolition metaphor a sign of imperial decline accompanied by escalating violence at home and abroad.

Trump does not issue the warning as a prophet might, that is, as an inspired utterance or overt injunction to heed the nation's democratic calling. His bluster is instead a reflection of "the sorrows of empire" and "dominion of war."[70] It signals a deeply troubled state of affairs in which Trump's rise is symptomatic and for which he offers no corrective other than an empty gesture to recovered greatness. Trump is no prophet, not even a false prophet. His disruptive persona and dismantlement motif, however, convey a latent prophecy, symbolically exposing an underlying sense of crisis.

The prophesy of the Trumpian tumult, in mythic terms, is apocalyptic. "Apocalypse means revelation," Northrop Frye observes, and the apocalyptic "reveals only on its own terms, and in its own forms," often in implicit or latent apocalyptic patterns.[71] It "shrouds its forecasts in mystery and ambiguity," James Darsey affirms, the language of which is "highly metaphorical and symbolic."[72] Apocalypse carries multiple meanings in U.S. political culture, with particular relevance to the mythos of American exceptionalism.[73] Richard Hughes characterizes the intertwining of the religious and the secular as a combined narrative of a chosen people comprising a Christian nation with a millennial mission, an innocent and righteous people opposed by the forces of evil.[74]

Apocalypse in both religious and secular variations signals a significant crisis, an impending catastrophe, a prophetic revelation, and a promise of salvation.[75] It may signify the collapse of civilization consistent with divine purpose or, in more secular terms, widespread destruction and devastation, such as visions of nuclear winter, global warming, economic collapse, and pandemic. The four horsemen of apocalypse are variously characterized as pestilence, war, famine, and death. Trump symbolizes the turmoil of imperial overreach, the crisis at hand. His demagoguery capitalizes on public discontent to protract rather than remediate imperialism.

In this way, Trump's metaphor of demolition, with its cathectic entailments, is a dumb instrument of prophetic disclosure, a true revelation of crisis but a false diagnosis of what is wrong and how best to respond. It reveals a crisis of empire that it does not recognize as an exigency for democratic vision. It testifies unknowingly to a critical moment, in Sheldon Wolin's terms, for disentangling from imperial commitments that have brought upon the nation endless war and for challenging the "inverted totalitarianism" of corporate power that exploits the authority and resources of the state to manage democracy and demobilize the citizenry. Democracy, Wolin insists, is "first and foremost about equality" made possible by "social cooperation." It is incompatible with "world domination."[76]

Trumpism troubles the nation's soul—vexes its vital center, its deepest convictions, its commitment to liberty, self-government, and equality. There was no assurance the luck of the past would keep a demagogue like Joe McCarthy from assuming the presidency, and it did not hold in 2016. Trump's mobilization of the nation's darker impulses, Jon Meacham avows, is a crisis that requires the people of the republic to call upon their better angels, to reach within the American soul for a guiding vision. The failings of the nation, the decay of injustice, tests a people's mettle to try anew. Hope looks to the future, even as fear of lost empire provokes anxiety, anger, and retrenchment. "Fear casts its eyes warily, even shiftily, across the landscape; hope looks forward, toward the horizon. Fear points at others, assigning blame; hope points ahead, working for a common good."[77]

Notes

1 Material in this chapter was first published as Robert L. Ivie and Oscar Giner, "Mythic Incantations of American Empire," *Res Rhetorica* 2, no. 2 (2015): 1–15, and Robert L. Ivie, "Trump's Unwitting Prophecy," *Rhetoric & Public Affairs* 20, no. 4 (2017): 707–17.
2 George Orwell, "Politics and the English Language," in *Marxism and Art*, ed. Berel Lang and Forrest Williams (1946; New York: David McKay Company, 1972), 433.
3 Friedrich Nietzsche, "On Truth and Lies in a Nonmoral Sense," in *Philosophy and Truth: Selections from Nietzsche's Notebooks of the Early 1870's*, ed. and trans. Daniel Breazeale (Amherst, NY: Humanity Books, 1999), 84–5.
4 Giambattista Vico, *New Science*, trans. David Marsh (1744; London: Penguin Books, 1999).
5 Kenneth Burke, *The Rhetoric of Religion* (Berkeley: University of California Press, 1970), 5, 236.

6 Kenneth Burke, *A Rhetoric of Motives* (1950; Berkeley: University of California Press, 1969), 265; José Martí, "Las Ruinas Indias," in *La Edad de Oro* (1889; México: Fondo de Cultura Económica, 1995), 265. The quotation from Martí is translated by Oscar Giner.
7 Mark Twain, "The United States of Lyncherdom," in *Collected Tales, Sketches, Speeches and Essays, 1891–1910*, ed. Louis J. Budd (New York: Library of America, 1992), 479.
8 Kenneth Burke, *Attitudes Toward History*, 3rd ed. (Berkeley: University of California Press, 1984), 166–75; Burke, *Rhetoric of Motives*, 19–23.
9 H. L. Mencken, "On Being an American," in *Prejudices: First, Second, and Third Series* (New York: The Library of America, 2010), 303–4.
10 *Holy Bible*, King James Version (Grand Rapids, MI: Zondervan Bible Publishers, 1984), Revelation 18:7; Matthew 23:27.
11 Walt Whitman, "Forrest as Gladiator," in *A Sourcebook in Theatrical History*, ed. A. M. Nagler (1846; New York: Dover Publications, 1952), 544–5.
12 Robert Montgomery Bird, "The Gladiator," in *Early American Drama*, ed. Jeffrey H. Richards (1831; New York: Penguin Books, 1997), 179–80.
13 Howard Fast, *Spartacus* (1951; New York: Bantam Books, 1960).
14 Kirk Douglas, *The Ragman's Son* (New York: Pocket Books, 1988), 294, 305.
15 Robert J. Lifton and Greg Mitchell, *Hiroshima in America: A Half Century of Denial* (New York: Avon Books, 1995), 337–40.
16 Fred Anderson and Andrew Cayton, *The Dominion of War: Empire and Liberty in North America, 1500–2000* (New York: Viking, 2005); Michael S. Sherry, *In the Shadow of War: The United States Since the 1930s* (New Haven, CT: Yale University Press, 1995); Kelly Denton-Borhaug, *U.S. War-Culture, Sacrifice and Salvation* (Sheffield, UK: Equinox, 2011). For a critique of the U.S. as a war state and war culture, written from a Chinese perspective and, ironically, projecting the same rhetorical imagery of a battle between barbarism and civilization (to prepare China for war with the U.S.) as has been used historically by the U.S. to justify its imperial wars, see Changming Liu, "US War Culture and the Destiny of the Empire," *International Critical Thought* 12, no. 3 (2022): 370–98.
17 Roger Stahl, *Militainment, Inc.: War, Media, and Popular Culture* (New York: Routledge, 2010).
18 Patrick Deer, "Mapping Contemporary American War Culture," *College Literature* 43, no. 1 (2016): 48–53, 56.
19 Henry A. Giroux, "War Culture and the Politics of Intolerable Violence," *Symplokē* 25, no. 1–2 (2017): 191–2, 194–7.
20 Richard T. Hughes, *Myths America Lives By* (Urbana: University of Illinois Press, 2003).
21 For a critical analysis of U.S. war in the name of peace, see Jon Simons, "The Invisibility of Liberal Peace: Perpetual Peace and Enduring Peace," in *In/visible War: The Culture of War in Twenty-First-Century America*, ed. Jon Simons and John Louis Lucaites (New Brunswick, NJ: Rutgers University Press, 2017), 213–28.
22 Deer, 66–8.
23 Aeschylus, *Oresteia*, trans. Richmond Lattimore (Chicago: University of Chicago Press, 1953), lines 119, 133.
24 Euripides, *Iphigeneia at Aulis*, trans. Richmond Lattimore (New York: Oxford University Press, 1973), lines 1611–13, 1710–12.

25 Robert L. Ivie, *Dissent from War* (Bloomfield, CT: Kumarian Press, 2007), 1.
26 Charles Krauthammer, "Obama vs. Putin: The Mismatch," *Washington Post*, March 27, 2014, https://www.washingtonpost.com/opinions/charles-krauthammer-obama-vs-putin-the-mismatch/2014/03/27/e26a27f2-b5d5-11e3-8cb6-284052554d74_story.html.
27 U.S. Department of State (2015), "The Terrorist Enemy" (2015), http://www.state.gov/j/ct/enemy/.
28 Spencer Ackerman, "'Apocalyptic' ISIS Beyond Anything We've Seen, Say US Defence Chiefs," *Guardian*, August 22, 2014, https://www.theguardian.com/world/2014/aug/21/isis-us-military-iraq-strikes-threat-apocalyptic.
29 Richard Cohen, "The Islamic State Is Evil Returned," *Washington Post*, August 25, 2014, https://www.washingtonpost.com/opinions/richard-cohen-the-islamic-state-is-evil-returned/2014/08/25/93eccd9c-2c85-11e4-9b98-848790384093_story.html.
30 Patrick Cockburn, "Iraq Crisis: Capture of Mosul Ushers in the Birth of a Sunni Caliphate," *The Independent*, June 11, 2014, https://www.independent.co.uk/voices/iraq-crisis-capture-of-mosul-ushers-in-the-birth-of-a-sunni-caliphate-9530600.html; David Ignatius, "The Return of al-Qaeda," *Washington Post*, June 10, 2014, https://www.washingtonpost.com/opinions/david-ignatius-the-return-of-al-qaeda/2014/06/10/4a82eaaa-f0ea-11e3-bf76-447a5df6411f_story.html.
31 Jessy J. Ohr, "In Pursuit of Light War in Libya: Kairotic Justification of War that Just Happened," *Rhetoric & Public Affairs* 20, no. 2 (2017): 196–7.
32 Michael M. Osborn, "The Evolution of the Archetypal Sea in Rhetoric and Poetic," *Quarterly Journal of Speech* 63, no. 4 (1977): 347–63.
33 Theodore Roosevelt, "Naval War College Address," June 2, 1897, http://www.theodore-roosevelt.com/trspeeches.html.
34 Jim Michaels, "Iraq Speeds Up Planned ISIL Counteroffensive," *USA Today*, December 4, 2014, https://www.usatoday.com/story/news/world/2014/12/04/iraq-counteroffensive-against-islamic-state/19858843/.
35 Liz Sly, "Al-Qaeda Group's Gains in Syria Undermine U.S. Strategy," *Washington Post*, December 5, 2014, https://www.washingtonpost.com/world/middle_east/al-qaeda-inspired-rebels-gain-in-syria-making-life-even-worse-for-us-allied-forces/2014/12/05/0930bde0-7388-11e4-95a8-fe0b46e8751a_story.html.
36 Barak Obama, "Remarks by the President at the National Defense University," *The White House*, Office of the Press Secretary, May 23, 2013, http://www.whitehouse.gov/the-press-office/2013/05/23/remarks-president-national-defense-university.
37 Shakespeare, "Macbeth," in *The Yale Shakespeare*, ed. Wilbur L. Cross and Tucker Brooke (New York: Barnes & Noble, 1993), 1.4.134–7.
38 Obama, "Remarks at National Defense University."
39 Shakespeare, Macbeth, 4.2.127.
40 Obama, "Remarks at National Defense University."
41 *Dirty Wars*, directed by Richard Rowley (New York, NY: Sundance Selects, 2015). DVD.
42 Joseph Campbell, *The Inner Reaches of Outer Space* (1986; Novato, CA: New World Library, 2002).
43 *Holy Bible*, New Revised Standard Version (New York: Oxford University Press, 1977), 1 Samuel 16:18.

44 *Holy Bible*, NRSV, 1 Samuel 17: 36.
45 Walter Pincus, "Islamic State's Bloody Message Machine," *Washington Post*, September 29, 2014, https://www.washingtonpost.com/world/national-security/islamic-states-bloody-message-machine/2014/09/29/29dc57b6-4598-11e4-b437-1a7368204804_story.html.
46 Carl Jung, "The Structure of the Psyche," in *The Portable Jung*, ed. Joseph Campbell (New York: Penguin Books, 1976), 39, 42, 44.
47 See Carl Jung, "The Archetypes and the Collective Unconsious," in *Collected Works of C.G. Jung* (Princeton, NJ: Princeton University Press, 1969), Vol. 9, Part 1.
48 Barack Obama, "Statement by the President on ISIL," September 10, 2014, *The White House*, Office of the Press Secretary, http://www.whitehouse.gov/the-press-office/2014/09/10/statement-president-isil-1.
49 Marlene Winnell and Valerie Tarico, "How Conservative Christianity Can Warp the Mind," *Alternet*, October 29, 2014, http://www.alternet.org/belief/how-conservative-christianity-can-warp-mind.
50 Kenneth Burke, *Language as Symbolic Action: Essays on Life, Literature, and Method* (Berkeley: University of California Press, 1968), 16–18, 155; Kenneth Burke, *Attitudes Toward History*, 3rd ed. (Berkeley: University of California Press, 1984), 422; Robert L. Ivie, "Kenneth Burke's Attitude Toward Rhetoric," *Rhetorica Scandinavica* 73 (June 2016): 17–18.
51 For a discussion of Trump's rhetoric of upheaval and his factionally tragic appeal intermixed with burlesque, see Edward C. Appel, "Burlesque, Tragedy, and a (Potentially) 'Yuuuge' 'Breaking of a Frame': Donald Trump's Rhetoric as 'Early Warning'?" *Communication Quarterly* 66, no. 2 (2018): 157–75.
52 Jason A. Edwards, "Make America Great Again: Donald Trump and Redefining the U.S. Role in the World," *Communication Quarterly* 66, no. 2 (2018): 177.
53 Mary E. Stuckey, "American Elections and the Rhetoric of Political Change: Hyperbole, Anger, and Hope in U.S. Politics," *Rhetoric & Public Affairs* 20, no. 4 (2017): 667–94.
54 Jennifer R. Merceica, "Dangerous Demagogues and Weaponized Communication," *Rhetoric Society Quarterly* 49, no. 3 (2019): 264–79.
55 Robert E. Terrill, "The Post-racial and Post-ethical Discourse of Donald J. Trump," *Rhetoric & Public Affairs* 20, no. 3 (2017): 501, 504–6.
56 Alison Hearn, "Trump's 'Reality' Hustle," *Television & New Media* 17, no. 7 (2016): 658.
57 Bonnie Dow, "Taking Trump Seriously: Persona and Presidential Politics in 2016," *Women's Studies in Communication* 40, no. 2 (2017): 136–8.
58 For an extended discussion of rhetoric and demagoguery, see Patricia Roberts-Miller, *Rhetoric and Demagoguery* (Carbondale: Southern Illinois University Press, 2019), and for a somewhat alternative take on demagoguery and democracy, see Ryan Skinnell, "Using Democracy against Itself: Democratic Rhetoric as an Attack on Democratic Institutions," *Rhetoric Society Quarterly* 49, no. 3 (2019): 248–63.
59 Mark Andrejevic, "The *Jouissance* of Trump," *Television & New Media* 17, no. 7 (2016): 651–2.
60 For an early and prescient take on contemporary media culture reducing news to stupefying entertainment, see Neil Postman, *Amusing Ourselves to Death: Public Discourse in the Age of Show Business* (New York: Viking, 1985).

61 Even chief strategist Stephen Bannon was subject to Trump's impulse to fire subordinates.
62 Kendall R. Phillips, "'The Safest Hands Are Our Own': Cinematic Affect, State Cruelty, and the Election of Donald J. Trump," *Communication and Critical/Cultural Studies* 15, no. 1 (2018): 85, 86–9. On the racist overtones of Trump's rhetoric, see also Robert L. Ivie, "Dissenting Democratically from Trump's Toxic Tropes," *Javnost–The Public* 30, no. 1 (2023): 1–17.
63 Brian L. Ott, "The Age of Twitter: Donald J. Trump and the Politics of Debasement," *Critical Studies in Media Communication* 34, no. 1 (2017): 63.
64 Donald J. Trump, "President Trump Rally Speech in Louisville, Kentucky, March 20, 2017." *Fox News*, https://www.youtube.com/watch?v=4a6zF2ya3c4.
65 Donald Trump, "President Donald Trump 100 Days Rally in Harrisburg, Pennsylvania, 4/29/2017: at Trump Live," https://www.youtube.com/watch?v=ICo39_Zuk9Q.
66 Trump, "Harrisburg Rally."
67 Donald J. Trump, "The Inaugural Address," January 20, 2017, *The White House*, Office of the Press Secretary, https://www.whitehouse.gov/inaugural-address.
68 Greg Jaffe and Jenna Johnson, "Trump Delights in Watching the U.S. Military Display Its Strength," *Washington Post*, April 14, 2017, https://www.washingtonpost.com/politics/trump-delights-in-watching-the-us-military-display-its-strength/2017/04/14/1f0e02a4-2113-11e7-ad74-3a742a6e93a7_story.html?utm_term=.c33f613b1eb7&wpisrc=nl_headlines&wpmm=1.
69 Donald J. Trump, "Remarks by President Trump in Joint Address to Congress," *The White House*, Office of the Press Secretary, February 28, 2017, https://www.whitehouse.gov/the-press-office/2017/02/28/remarks-president-trump-joint-address-congress.
70 Chalmers Johnson, *The Sorrows of Empire: Militarism, Secrecy, and the End of the Republic* (New York: Metropolitan Books, 2004); Fred Anderson and Andrew Cayton, *The Dominion of War: Empire and Liberty in North America, 1500–2000* (New York: Viking, 2005).
71 Northrop Frye, *Anatomy of Criticism* (Princeton, NJ: Princeton University Press, 1957), 125, 139, 158.
72 James Darsey, *The Prophetic Tradition and Radical Rhetoric in America* (New York: New York University Press, 1997), 118.
73 See, for instance, Andrew J. Bacevich, *American Empire* (Cambridge, MA: Harvard University Press, 2002); Andrew J. Bacevich, *The New American Militarism: How Americans Are Seduced by War* (New York: Oxford University Press, 2005); Andrew J. Bacevich, *The Limits of Power: The End of American Exceptionalism* (New York: Henry Holt and Company, 2008).
74 Richard T. Hughes, *Myths America Lives By* (Urbana: University of Illinois Press, 2003), 5–8.
75 David Adams Leeming, *The World of Myth* (New York: Oxford University Press, 1990), 76–7.
76 Sheldon S. Wolin, *Democracy Incorporated* (Princeton, NJ: Princeton University Press, 2008), xii, xvi–xviii, xxi, 44–7, 52–3, 56–7, 61.
77 Jon Meacham, *The Soul of America: The Battle for Our Better Angels* (New York: Random House, 2018), 6–9, 13, 270–1.

· 3 ·

VETERAN'S LAMENT[1]

War culture, as a naturalized discourse, is indisposed to change. It is entrenched, inflexible, and seemingly immutable, its inertia largely undisturbed by other influences and extraneous factors.[2] Fixed resilience, though, eventually diminishes its capacity to adjust to challenge and change. Fissures open and widen; rigidity occasions instability. Internal pressure builds. Underlying tensions expose the artificiality of a naturalized discursive formation. War culture becomes increasingly subject to intervention and transformation.[3]

There is good reason to approach war as a cultural construct and to consider its discursive instability. As Adam Hodges observes, "Humans never engage in war without the mediating force of discourse."[4] Discursive processes create enemies, mobilize fighting forces, and structure memories that glorify and mythologize warfare. War, as suggested by anthropological evidence, is a culturally contingent phenomenon.[5] Just as humans are socialized to kill, they can be socialized to promote peace.[6] "Discursive practices," Hodges submits, "constitute a central means by which culturally specific systems of meaning—including the moral values important in a given society—are brought into existence."[7] Discursive practices that instantiate war, unless they are contested, can habituate society to institutionalized militarism.

Language is socially and politically constitutive; its constructions necessarily are mutable. As Lene Hansen puts the matter, "The ambiguous nature of language as both structured and unstable implies that discourses will try to construct themselves as stable, but that there will always be slips and instabilities." The ongoing discursive process of "linking and differentiation" entails the "possibility for destabilization."[8] Hence, what we know of national security at any given point in time is open potentially to re-articulation and reinterpretation.

For the most part, war culture is what we know and experience; a culture of peace is what we imagine. Both are discursively conceived and constituted. As Boulding observes, each is an "ideal" type, a "pure form" that is never perfectly realized; "societies tend to be a blend of peaceful and warrior culture themes," even though "peaceableness" is under-reported compared to violence. "The deeply held belief that war is a basic, inevitable, and divinely ordained process in human history" will change "only with a much wider recognition of the actual peace processes at work in every society."[9] Human beings are neither basically violent nor inevitably peaceful, writes Steven Pinker, but they can be impelled toward compassion, fairness, reason, and peace.[10]

Hence, Barak Obama sets out to change the U.S. mindset of war. He reaches the threshold of a new democratic sensibility but is held back by war culture's strong gravitational pull. His effort is not without consequence, however. He unsettles the narrow American identity on which U.S. empire bases its claim to white exceptionalism. While empire's mythic landscape of dead metaphors seems impervious to change because it hides its fractures, seals its cracks, and fills its gaps to appear naturalized and inevitable, its cumulative rigidity makes repair increasingly difficult until finally an outburst of raw demagoguery portends its collapse. Even the mythical authority of the warrior is subject to appropriation for the purpose of constructing an attitude of peace. Veterans advocating for peace expose the tension existing within war culture and signal the potential for a paradigm shift. Thus, we turn our attention now to repurposing the warrior myth.

Warrior Myth

"I regard myself as a soldier, though a soldier of peace."

Mahatma Gandhi, 1931[11]

Myth, trope, discourse, and political culture are intertwined. Myth is a permeating pattern, "*a symbolic story of the whole*—the whole system, thing, person, practice, polity, culture, or the like," writes John Nelson.[12] Tropes convey a dynamic sense of mythic vision as they turn language to reframe thought. Within the mythic dimension of war culture resides an incipient discourse of peace. The twist of the warrior myth resonates with a legacy of resistance to the cult of the kill. A liminal sensibility, rendered here in poetic interludes 1–4, is the immanent cultural context underpinning a transformation of warriors into soldiers of peace. Our poetic mediations gesture to the mythic overtones of prophetic dissonance in the veteran's dissent. As a discourse of reform, prophecy goads a reluctant people to realign themselves with sacred principles.[13]

The figure of the soldier carries mythic force in political discourse.[14] The warrior myth is ancient and enduring. It represents soldiers as fearless fighters, saviors performing heroic deeds. The hero archetype links the personal to the collective and the past to the present. The hero's quest is a divinely enabled struggle against monstrous foes in pursuit of enlightenment and spiritual atonement.[15]

The ethos of the nation—its character, guiding beliefs, and moral sentiments—is invested in the persona of the heroic soldier. This is decidedly true of the United States. The U.S. soldier signifies patriotism, courage, sacrifice, and faith in the nation's sacred mission.[16] Public rituals in support of the troops permeate popular culture and political discourse. The uniformed soldier is featured at sporting events large and small. The President's annual State of the Union speech spotlights military heroes. The tomb of the Unknown Soldier symbolizes the warrior's ultimate sacrifice. These political rituals and monuments (with partial exceptions such as the Vietnam Veterans Memorial) reconstitute Americans as a people in the image of the warrior. Just as soldier-citizens fight for the nation and its constituting ideal, patriotic ceremonies identifying the people with their fallen heroes represent war as the nation's transcendent purpose.[17] The soldier embodies the myth of redemptive violence—that killing secures the nation and preserves what is good in the world—and personifies "the ultimate duty for American citizens."[18]

The state equates loyalty to the soldier with support for war, a semiotic merger in which questioning any war implies disrespecting every soldier—past, present, and future. The mythic authority of the warrior is reassuring when it conforms to the rule of militarism (that war is an instrument of peace) and unsettling when, in telling an opposing story of imperial misadventure, it diverges from the conventional wisdom of the war state.[19] Veterans challenging the conceits of war create cultural dissonance.

Preferring to hear itself exalted by battle-tested warriors, the nation retreats from the veteran's dissonant lament. The experience of war "exposes the lies we tell ourselves about ourselves," including that one nation is virtuous above others and that wars are noble. Americans routinely ascribe their own "capacity for evil" to their enemies. They do not want to acknowledge that war up close is "a soulless void," that it is "about barbarity, perversion and pain, an unchecked orgy of death," that it crushes human decency, or that "the noise, the stench, the fear, the scenes of eviscerated bodies and bloated corpses, the cries of the wounded" constitute the "moral void" of combat.[20] Veterans who speak this painful truth—that the essence of war is death—are more often ignored, even condemned, than applauded because what they say as prophets is difficult to digest. Still, their prophetic voices cannot be dismissed entirely—they are too potent a signifier of valor—without a collective twinge of conscience. Dissenting soldiers are a crack in the patriotic façade of militarism.

This point of cultural tension—the incongruity of the veteran soldier opposed to militarism—warrants attention for what it can reveal about the symbolic resources of transformation residing within discourses of war. It provides an opportunity to examine a critique from within that converts the terminology of war into a vehicle of peace. Converted to the ends of peacemaking, the warrior myth lends a heroic sensibility, a measure of credibility, a foundation for reason, an overtone of action, and a feeling of viability to a vision of peace that otherwise seems naive, implausible, passive, and hazardous. The figure of the warrior becomes a vehicle of cultural innovation that prefigures a possibility of change, a way of imagining an end to interminable warfare on the demons endemic to U.S. war culture.[21]

Mediation 1: The Fate of Prometheus

Like ancient rumors trapped in a cultural heritage, veteran voices call out from a magic well of lived experiences. They are (in Calderón de la Barca's phrase) "allegorical ghosts without time or place," pointing to a road not taken.[22] The path they herald can be constructed only with willful steps, blow by blow, guided by their distant voices, seemingly buried under the cacophony of modern political discourse and war posturing.

The first one in Greek mythology to stand against the rule of tyrants was Prometheus. Before the oceans were born, before land altered into matter, he betrayed his own race and enlisted in the army of young gods who fought a war against the Titans. Prometheus helped set up the tyranny of the "new and terrible lords of Olympos," and was later tortured and imprisoned by them.[23]

He taught humankind the arts of civilization. He stole fire from the gods, hiding the spark in a fennel stalk, and carried it aloft as a gift to humanity. He had compassion for the "suffering race" of mortals for which Zeus cared nothing. By his own account, Zeus "planned to wipe out the whole species and breed another, a new one."[24]

As soon as Prometheus turned against the privilege of the gods, he was arrested, beaten and vilified. Power and Force brought him to a cliff. Hephaistos, the crippled god of fire renowned for his metallurgy, reluctantly (for Prometheus was brother and friend) chained him to a rock, fettered his wrists, shackled his legs, and locked iron bands around his rib cage.

This is the usual way. With their credentials and legitimacy, veterans who reject war threaten the system of violence and plunder. Like Prometheus, they are branded traitors and punished swiftly. The nation is complicit in the violence of its rulers.

Veterans for Peace

The members of Veterans for Peace (VFP)—an organization founded in 1985 to increase public awareness of the costs of war—were alert to the tension generated by soldiers criticizing the war system. Jerry Genesio, VFP's first president, observed that, while opposing the foreign policy of one's country can be perceived as subversive, informing audiences of his service in the Marine Corps rendered them attentive and respectful even when they disagreed with him. His credibility as a soldier made it more difficult, but not impossible, to question his patriotism.[25]

VFP members drew upon their attenuated credibility as warriors to launch a critique of war as the "demon that has slaughtered untold millions." Rather than believe official claims about "malevolent forces" threatening the national wellbeing, they insisted, the public should listen to the cautionary tales of military veterans with "knowledge of war and war preparations." They were exercising their "patriotic duty" once again, this time to ensure that

U.S. foreign policy upheld "the highest principles of international law and humanitarianism."²⁶

Mediation 2: St. Ignatius at Manresa

God "takes fishermen as the instruments and preachers of the light of his Gospel and his truth in order to confuse the world, and to show that He is Lord and that He works wonders ... and that He is not like the princes and kings of the century, who can grant the office as they say, but not the discretion or necessary talents to do it justice."²⁷

Much of VFP's persuasive effort was aimed at erasing the "image of the enemy." Toward that end, they personalized the "so-called enemy." Their aim was to educate the public on "the human, social, and economic effects of war," hoping that their special credibility would enable them "to project the voice of dissent."²⁸ They lifted their voices in support of a culture of peace—exposing the costs of war, working to heal the wounds of war, resisting intervention in the internal affairs of other countries, and seeking the elimination of nuclear weapons, an end to the arms race, and the rejection of war as an instrument of national policy.²⁹

Fact-Finding Mission to Nicaragua

VFP undertook a fact-finding mission to Central America in 1987 to challenge the veracity of the Reagan administration's claim that a Sandinista revolution in Nicaragua threatened U.S. security. Genesio had traveled to Nicaragua previously with his wife as members of a Witness for Peace delegation. On that trip in 1984, they met with government officials and opposition leaders and shared meals with families living inside the combat zone. "Humanity cannot be neatly divided into camps of friends and enemies," Genesio concluded, because "we are all members of the same species ... with the same basic wants, needs and emotions. ...We cannot continue killing our children as a means of resolving our conflicts."³⁰ The trip revealed that the Sandinista government had achieved significant social progress in its first five years, including major strides in healthcare, literacy, housing, environmental protection, and land reform. The Reagan administration's military support of the rightwing Contra war seemed immoral and indefensible to Genesio and his fellow witnesses for peace.

The 1987 VFP fact-finding mission to Nicaragua arrived first in Guatemala, which Reagan had depicted as an exemplary new democracy. VFP encountered instead the extreme poverty of a peasant class victimized by criminals, power elites, the police, and the military in what amounted essentially to "a neo-fascist military police state." The situation they found in Nicaragua was different. VFP fact finders discovered a Nicaraguan people they described as "friendly, open, and warm," people who "spoke proudly and supportively of the Sandinista revolution and government." In less than eight years, the Sandinista government had opened free health clinics in every city, town, and village. Polio was eradicated. People were being treated for malaria. Over 1,500 schools had been built. Deep wells were dug and sewer systems installed to provide peasants with safe water. While the Sandinistas had worked to improve the lives of the Nicaraguan people, the U.S.-supported Contra war had left in its wake tens of thousands of orphans, destroyed millions of dollars of emergency medical and food supplies, devastated rice, bean, and coffee crops, damaged schools, churches, health facilities, utilities, and granaries, and terrorized the population with random kidnappings, executions, and mutilations. Reagan's proxy war had "inflicted an incredible amount of needless human suffering," the delegation concluded.[31]

Humanizing the People of Iraq

VFP's goal of humanizing the enemy—of making war, not the foreign other, the demon—was reflected in the efforts of one of its members to teach the lesson of a wrongful war in Iraq. "Whatever success this book has will be measured by the extent to which readers begin to see [the 24 million people of Iraq] as fellow human beings," wrote Mike Ferner, a member of Veterans for Peace and author of *Inside the Red Zone*.[32] The Red Zone was all of Iraq outside of the heavily fortified, 3.9 square-mile Green Zone in central Baghdad, headquarters for the U.S. occupation. Ferner spent a month in Iraq in 2003, just prior to the U.S. invasion, and returned for two months a year later.

Ferner focused attention on everyday people to make the point that Iraq did not reduce to Saddam Hussein. This was his way of countering U.S. war propaganda that mobilized public opinion by featuring the image of an evil dictator. He did not defend Iraq's dictator when, for example, a radio show host—"sitting in the comfort of his downtown Toledo [Ohio] studio"—asked rhetorically if "sometimes ruthless thugs have to be dealt with ... [if] we sometimes just have to go in and take care of things?" Calling in to the show from Baghdad, Ferner responded by asking, "Just who should we take care of ... Should it be Ahmed, the kid who shined my shoes this morning, or Kamil, the hotel's tea-room manager who talked with me last night, or Mohammed, our cab driver today?"[33]

Taking out the evil dictator would mean endangering the lives of regular people like Khalid, a cab driver who despised Saddam Hussein but did not want war, or Mr. Al-Nasseb, a high school math teacher who wryly remarked that the Iraqi dictator had been exchanged for U.S. imperialism. Jacob Joseph, an administrator at a Baghdad high school, acknowledged that Saddam Hussein was "a beast and a monster" and said he "wanted to get rid of him." But, he observed, "The Americans created Saddam Hussein and the Americans got rid of Saddam Hussein," leaving the Iraqi people without jobs and living amidst devastation that spawned terrorism.[34] The actual victims of a war to remove Saddam Hussein were the people of Iraq. Humanizing stories of and by everyday people resisted the Bush administration's demonizing rhetoric by telling readers "that Iraqis are indeed just like us."[35]

To drive home this identification of Iraqis with Americans, Ferner featured the voices of Iraqi school children. Their letters to American students expressed personal interests in soccer, music, and computers, making them and their criticism of the U.S. occupation less alien. Rami, a teenager who liked playing sports, using computers, and "hanging out with friends," wrote that "nobody dares to go out" after 10:00 p.m. and before 7:00 a.m., when "only robbers or American soldiers are seen in the streets." Bashar, a 16-year-old "middle child" with an older brother and younger sister, wrote that it is not "a matter of Saddam having or not having mass destruction weapons." With or without them, the "USA was never threatened by Iraq, except in pretending of American administration." Ahmed, who loved soccer, actor Mel Gibson, and actress Michelle Pfeiffer, allowed that "Saddam Hussein was not a very good man but, however, he is better than those who are governing the country right now." Wael loved swimming and music, but not Bush or Saddam. She thought the war was "a very big mistake. ... But tell me," she wrote to Brandon, "what do you think about Beyonce."[36]

Ferner also published photographs of children living, suffering, and dying under U.S. occupation. Four village children peered apprehensively through a window blown out by a cruise missile strike on a nearby orange grove. A child screamed after U.S. soldiers killed her parents and seriously wounded her brother. A father grieved over the bodies of three of his children laid out in an open casket—three dead children among 33 civilians killed and 310 wounded in a coalition bombing raid on a residential area.[37]

Ordinary Iraqi adults professed to be neither with the U.S. president nor for the terrorists. "Is this the democracy of civilized people in the U.S., to kill innocent human beings with no reason?" asked Sheik Khalid Hussain on behalf of "simple people and farmers." In prosecuting a war against the Iraqi people, suggested a man named Faris, "what has been achieved is very fragile."[38] Americans should put their faith in democracy instead of war.

Peace at Home, Peace Abroad

The devastating invasion of Iraq in 2003, during which VFP expanded to over 8,000 members, focused the organization's attention on "the endless global war on terror."[39] VFP working groups addressed issues of drone warfare, depleted uranium weapons, cluster bombs, landmines, war crimes, post-traumatic stress disorder, and more.[40] VFP position statements were written on "The Iraq Debacle," "The 11th Anniversary of the U.S. Invasion of Afghanistan," "No U.S. Military Intervention in Syria," among other topics.[41] From 2009 to 2014, VFP published a quarterly newspaper, "War Crimes Times."[42] "Only by owning up to the mindless failure of U.S. military efforts since 9/11," observed VFP Advisory Board Member and history professor Andrew J. Bacevich, "does it become possible to restore real choice. Alternatives to open-ended war waged on the other side of the globe do exist."[43]

VFP released a position paper in 2014 that framed its mission under the banner of "Peace at Home, Peace Abroad." Moving toward a culture of peace, the paper argued, required recognizing that "the violence of war has been epidemic [in the U.S.] since its founding." This was a "new lens" for seeing that "everything is connected" when it comes to waging peace. Domestic attitudes and policy are connected to militarism and foreign policy. Domestic "racism," in particular, is "a driving force for modern war." Dehumanizing terms such as "'haji,' 'towel head,' 'gook' and 'sand-nigger'"—"used to brainwash us into fighting and killing"—poison the well of human solidarity.[44] Ending war, VAP argued, requires "an all-encompassing demand for peace," which includes ending racism, oppression, poverty, lack of universal health care, environmental degradation, and more.[45]

Honoring the Soldier's Sacrifice

An affiliated group of dissenting veterans, Iraq Veterans Against the War, was founded in 2004 at the annual VFP convention. IVAW gave voice to recent veterans and active duty servicemen and servicewomen "under various pressures to remain silent."[46] Organizing members believed that support for war among soldiers was a vulnerable pillar of the war system.[47] IVAW would "address veterans, active-duty troops, followed by journalists and historians, antiwar groups and other allies, and policymakers," largely in that order, with the goal of educating the public about the realities of the Iraq war.[48] The soldiers' experiential knowledge added texture and a degree of moral authority to challenge the war system. "There's nothing like actually being an occupier in a foreign country to make you finally realize that foreign policy affects you directly," testified IVAW founder, Kelly Dougherty.[49]

Mediation 3: Philoctetes Protests

Left behind on the Island of Lemnos by the Greeks on their sea voyage to Troy, Philoctetes hangs upside down on the tree of sacrifice. He speaks the words of all wounded warriors, the silent monologue which is the legacy of all wars.

"If the kingdom of God is within you, so is the kingdom of Hell. I have seen more than I can speak. ...Through it all I followed the flag. *The flag!*

I once baptized unbelievers in the rivers of Asia. I wore a sacred amulet, which I lost in a firefight and later found it around the neck of an Asian boy. I offered him a chocolate bar in trade for it, threatened him with my M16, and took it back from him because I felt vulnerable without it.

They told me that if I hang on this withered tree Resurrection will follow, but I suspect that was only another lie. I sacrificed for country, but there was no country where I went, and no country left when I came back—only those around me, who sacrificed as well.

Only before the Wall can I commune with them, and yet they never cross over. Only at the Wall before their names do I find relief.

Bound hand and foot I hang from the ash tree, where Odin learned to read the runes. I cannot tell whether wisdom or knowledge will come from the scar in my left eye. I'm told that New Life stirs within me, and sometimes I sense a golden glow around my head. But I am lost in melancholy, buried by inertia, driven to despair.

I cannot see Mary Magdalene, but I feel her near. Little children play around me, throwing stones as they pass in play. I do not mind them. I like their laughter and stories.

Oh the horror! The pain of glory, the wound at the heart of the sacrifice!

Offering roses dipped in blood to the sun, a warrior in battle with an alligator of pain, the sole object of this station is survival, to win a place in the Lodge of Sun Dancers. The yearning of Mary Magdalene keeps me alive; at the foot of the cross, the love of Mary Magdalene.

In darkness I am questioned among lights and shadows (I followed the *flag!*). I cannot speak of the dead, or mention the mud and rain, the desert sand in mouth and nostrils, the icy, shark-infested waters, the spreading ooze of blackened oil, the burning ironclads and sinking aircraft carriers. The firebird plunges from the sky in a downward spiral; the earth receives it like a mother caressing the corpse of a child on her lap. My yell is silent; it resembles the howl of an animal, unable or unwilling to escape from the trap.

Two robbers on opposite sides of the Crucified One: the first one says if you're so great, so brave and bold a hero, why don't you free yourself, you fraud, you coward, and you clown? The second one says he was better than we were. He followed something, sacrificed for someone. Why berate him?

I can't escape the memories. Darkness blinds me now. But my voice will reach all corners."[50]

Implicitly channeling this poetic vision of an exiled mythic hero, IVAW organized a four-day Winter Soldier event explicitly for U.S. veterans to testify publicly to their experiences as occupiers in Iraq and Afghanistan.[51] Dozens recounted stories of "killing innocent civilians, randomly seizing and torturing prisoners, refusing to treat injured Afghans and Iraqis, looting, taking 'trophy' photos of the dead, and falsifying reports to make it look as though civilians they killed were actually 'insurgents.'"[52] Their testimony revealed how military occupation leads to "racism, dehumanization, and sexism directed both outward at the enemy and inward into the soul of the service member."[53] The March 2008 event contributed to a critical discussion of key issues by documenting a systematic "disregard for the rules of engagement, dehumanization of the enemy, and breakdown of the military."[54]

The Iraq war was unjust from IVAW's standpoint.[55] A just society would care for its warrior's needs better, hold political leaders, profiteers, and war criminals accountable, and emphasize alternatives to militarism.[56] IVAW envisioned a political culture of nonviolence, open communication, democratic decision-making, human solidarity, and working toward reconciliation of differences. It argued for peacemaking instead of warfare as the best way to honor the soldier's sacrifice.

Soldiers of Peace

Focusing on the evil of war (its essence of destruction and death), humanizing the image of the designated enemy (recognizing the innocent victims of warfare), acknowledging a history of militarism, racism, and structural injustice (looking inward instead of projecting outward), committing to nonviolent advocacy, democratic decision-making, and diplomacy (reconciling rather than suppressing differences)—these are the themes of the veteran's prophetic voice calling on the nation to wage peace instead of war. They express a vision of transcending the myth of war's inevitability and transforming the warrior into a soldier of peace, a vision amplified by Paul Chappell (a West Point graduate) into a discourse of peacemaking articulated in a military idiom.

Chappell reworked the language of war and adapted the image of the warrior to infuse nonviolent means and ends with a heroic sensibility. He contested the belief in war's inevitability, typically grounded in the archetypal image of human instinct that naturalizes war and makes the idea of peacemaking appear naïve. "The myth that humans are naturally violent," he insisted, is wrongheaded and freighted with "devastating consequences." Rather than being biologically programmed to kill one another, humans innately resist killing other human beings—a truth, Chappell argued, that is clearly reflected in the fact that, to wage war, propagandists have to dehumanize enemies and caricature them as evil. The biggest challenge of any army is to keep soldiers from fleeing the battlefield. Soldiers prefer to posture than fight, to frighten away adversaries rather than engage them in combat. Bravery in combat, when it occurs, is motivated by compassion (not hate), by a desire to protect the lives of loved ones, including one's fellow soldiers. Human survival requires "a bond powerful enough to hold a community together and to encourage selfless service, sacrifice, and cooperation among its members." Cooperation motivated by a concern for the wellbeing of others is "not a naïve moral virtue but a crucial survival instinct," which can serve the ends of peacemaking.[57]

Mediation 4: The Baptist of An Hoa

Vietnam, 1968. Lee Benjamin arrived two weeks after the Tet Offensive. At the age of 19, he found himself a young Marine at the siege of Khe Sanh, a Jew among Christians:

> But I did not baptize anyone in Khe Sanh. I wouldn't go out of the sandbagged holes we lived in much because they could sniper at you. I took only 11 showers in 4–5 months, 4 of them while I was in the hospital with malaria.[58]

At An Hoa, his fellow grunts had "freaked." The company had gone in with about 150 troops and only 70 were left—some dead, some wounded, some poisoned by tree insects. They had been told by preachers, ministers, and chaplains that if they died in battle unbaptized they would go to Hell. Lee came from an upper middle-class white Jewish family in San Diego. He attributed this fear of damnation to the ignorance of uneducated young draftees. But he was a Forward Air Control guy and needed their protection in battle. Characteristically, he took direct and efficient action to address the situation:

> I can baptize you, if you want me to.
> How can you baptize if you are not a real priest or minister?
> I have special powers. I'm a Jew. John the Baptist was a Jew. I can baptize.

Several of his fellow Marines consented. What was there to lose?

Lee took them down to the river for the ceremony. There was one difficulty: he was not familiar with the Christian rite of Baptism. Praying to be shown the way, he laid hands on the head of each soldier and doused each one of them with water. He recited the Sabbath prayers for the blessing of candles. Guessing that some words in Latin were appropriate, he solemnly intoned the only words he remembered from history lessons about Julius Caesar: "*Vini, vidi, vici.*" To round off the ceremony, he pronounced each one of his comrades born again in the Grace of the Lord: "Man, you are baptized. Keep the faith baby and let's get short."

How exquisitely American to send poor young men to fight rich men's wars, to appeal to their patriotism in the face of bullets, explosives, and death in battle, and then to threaten them with Hell if they are not baptized! But the Baptist of An Hoa, risen from green river waters, armed his fellow soldiers with the Shield of Grace and the Promise of Salvation.

Captain Chappell—veteran of the U.S. war in Iraq—left active duty in 2009 to become a soldier of peace because, he maintained, war does not end by itself and peace cannot be achieved unless someone makes it happen. He marked "a path away from war" that channels "the warrior spirit toward peace."[59] The pursuit of peace requires "a paradigm shift," according to Chappell, to see true peace as a condition of "liberty, justice, opportunity, fairness, environmental sustainability, and other ingredients that create a healthy society."[60]

Chappell insisted that the pursuit of true peace is no more idealistic or less realistic than the challenge of fighting a war. "The Army knows that realistic idealists are powerful human beings capable of overcoming unimaginable odds, and that is why it trains its soldiers to be idealistic." Soldiers "rely on cooperation and solidarity to survive," which requires empathy, the ability to recognize one's self in another. "By cultivating empathy in its soldiers, the army is able to take people from different racial, social, religious, political, and economic backgrounds and forge bonds of friendship and family between them." We learn to see the humanity in others by hearing their stories.[61] Thus, soldiers of peace must rely on empathy to achieve solidarity locally, nationally, and globally in an interconnected world. Self-control, strategic planning, persistence in the face of adversity, confronting fear with a positive purpose—these are the key traits of a soldier ethos engaged in the mental martial art of waging peace.

Chappell took a cue from Mahatma Gandhi on the soldier ethos and the notion of channeling the warrior spirit toward waging peace. Peter Brock, observed Chappell, noted that Gandhi, especially in his later writings, showed respect for the positive qualities of heroism, comradeship, and duty that war brings out in everyday men. Gandhi, Brock reported, "would seek to create a technique that would preserve the virtues of the warrior while eliminating the negative aspects of warfare."[62] Like Sun Tzu (the ancient Chinese general and military strategist), Chappell argued, Gandhi believed we must know our enemies in order to engage them effectively, "but where waging peace is concerned the only way to truly know our enemies is by understanding and empathizing with them," in which case "they cease being our enemies and we can see them for who they truly are: fellow human beings held hostage by fear, hatred, or misunderstanding."[63]

In Chappell's paradigm of security, waging real peace requires developing a foreign policy grounded in respect—one in which the U.S. embraces freedom, democracy, and justice and leads by example in an interconnected world. Real peace entails addressing the underlying problems, such as poverty and lack of opportunity, that cause violent conflicts. Real peace involves strengthening international law against dictatorships and corruption rather than supporting brutal dictatorships in the name of spreading democracy and protecting freedom. Real peace engages international police work to combat terrorism as a crime instead of invading countries.[64]

In the spirit of a mythical trickster, Chappell crossed settled conceptual boundaries to intermix the meaning of war and peace.[65] He appropriated to peacemaking the age-old knowledge of war fighting. He deliberately misapplied the traditional warrior ethos, a reorientation consistent with Kenneth Burke's notion of perspective by incongruity, to produce a paradigm shift "by the merging of categories once felt to be mutually exclusive."[66] Like Prometheus, Chappell stole fire from the gods to give to humans the gift of civilization.

An Emergent Image

A paradigm shift can help to transcend the alienation of war. At a minimum, Kenneth Burke observes, transcendence can have a "contemplative effect" that permits the consideration of intense conflicts with less agitation.[67] The transformation of the warrior myth by veterans advocating for peace is neither a complete nor flawless achievement, but it is a noteworthy twist of war culture. To expect perfection, even compatibility with every aim of a positive peace, or to focus only on the limitations of the metaphor of "waging peace," is to ignore the trope's potential as an agent of transition. The democratic way, Burke observed, is to "muddle through," not being overly exact, making up specific policies "as one goes along, in accordance with the unforeseen newnesses that occur in the course of events, instead of approaching one's problem with an entire program laid out rigidly in advance."[68]

The gendered metaphor of "waging peace" is an unstable construction that can revert to the mindset of militarism or move beyond it. The metaphor conveys the tenor of peace in a linguistic vehicle that is commonly but ambiguously associated with combat, which affords an opportunity for restructuring conventional wisdom. Vico understood that culture is constituted and reconstituted in myth and that metaphors, as myths in miniature, are linguistic expressions of ingenium; they generate meaning that develops into knowledge.[69] In Burke's words, "By deliberate coaching and criticism of the perspective process, characters can be considered tentatively, in terms of other characters, for experimental or heuristic purposes," a process in which terms interact with one another to produce a fuller development of thought and attitude.[70]

"Waging peace" is an emergent image for redirecting the mythic force of the archetypal warrior. It is a figure of transition that gestures toward a plausible pursuit of life after empire, of living with diversity instead of continuing to combat it. It translates the courage and discipline of embattled warriors into the heroics of preventing warfare. Short of a complete narrative of peace building, the trope provides a culturally inflected incentive, a vantage point from which to assay militarism.

Beyond that, an incipient perspective of waging peace requires more than a rhetorical trickster's comic corrective to displace the god of war. In mythic terms, it takes a guiding star, an emblem of democratic revelation emerging amid spiritual turbulence, to create a new god and pursue a new direction. The opportunity for heightened consciousness, altered understanding, and a fresh beginning, occurring in a circumstance of crisis, follows from an internal struggle to break bad habits and part ways with a troubled identity. Only then, after letting go of familiar but tainted ways of being, is it possible to constitute and consult a culture's better angels. Such is the story of Genesis after which Old Man Coyote's work begins anew.

Notes

1. Material in this chapter was first published as Robert L. Ivie and Oscar Giner, "Waging Peace: Transformations of the Warrior Myth by U.S. Military Veterans," *Journal of Multicultural Discourses* 11, no. 2 (2016): 199–213.
2. For a study of the normalization of war in public culture from a visual perspective, see Jon Simons and John Louis Lucaites, eds. *In/visible War: The Culture of War in Twenty-First-Century America* (New Brunswick, NJ: Rutgers University Press, 2017). In their introduction to the volume, Simons and Lucaites observe that the multifaceted "paradox of the in/visibility of war" in the twenty-first century is "a public culture in which war is continuous and altogether present, but largely unseen and/or acknowledged. Indeed, awareness of and anxiety over persistent military conflict is displaced and normalized. The task, they argue, is to show in "a normalized war culture" what is *"already visible and yet remains unseen"* (2–3, 10; emphasis in original).
3. Roger Stahl, for instance, interrogates the standard presentation of war as a "weaponized gaze" that naturalizes war, rendering it a culturally habituated way of seeing. Stahl looks for openings in this naturalized discourse where vulnerabilities and pressure points might be exploited to subvert the weaponized gaze and promote public deliberation: Roger Stahl,

Through the Crosshairs: War, Visual Culture, and the Weaponized Gaze (Newark, NJ: Rutgers University Press, 2018).

4 Adam Hodges, "War, Discourse, and Peace," in *Discourses of War and Peace*, ed. Adam Hodges (New York: Oxford University Press, 2013), 3.

5 R. Brian Ferguson, "Archaeology, Cultural Anthropology, and the Origins and Intensification of War," in *The Archaeology of Warfare: Prehistories of Raiding and Conquest*, ed. Elizabeth N. Arkush and Mark W. Allen (Gainesville: University Press of Florida, 2006), 469–523; R. Brian Ferguson, "Ten Points on War," *Social Analysis* 52, no. 2 (2008): 32–49.

6 Douglas Fry, *The Human Potential for Peace: An Anthropological Challenge to Assumptions about War and Violence* (New York: Oxford University Press, 2006).

7 Adam Hodges, "War, Discourse, and Peace," 5.

8 Lene Hansen, *Security as Practice: Discourse Analysis and the Bosnian War* (London: Routledge, 2006), 20–1.

9 Elise Boulding, *Cultures of Peace: The Hidden Side of History* (Syracuse, NY: Syracuse University Press, 2000), 28.

10 Steven Pinker, *The Better Angels of Our Nature: Why Violence Has Declined* (New York: Viking, 2011), 482–3.

11 Mahatma Gandhi, "Speech to Women's International League for Peace and Freedom," December 10, 1931, Victoria Hall, Geneva, Switzerland. For an audio excerpt with the exact words, http://www.nonviolent-resistance.info/exhibitions/eng/gandhi/pg39.htm; for a text of the address, https://www.peacewomen.org/content/mathma-gandhi-address-wilpf-meeting-geneva-1931.

12 John S. Nelson, *Tropes of Politics: Science Theory, Rhetoric, Action* (Madison: University of Wisconsin Press, 1998), 157. Emphasis in original.

13 James Darsey, *The Prophetic Tradition and Radical Rhetoric in America* (New York: New York University Press, 1997), 16.

14 The term "soldier" is used in a broad sense, as an expression of convenience, to refer to those who serve in the various military services, not just the army. To quote Nan Levinson [*War Is Not a Game: The New Antiwar Soldiers and the Movement They Built* (New Brunswick, NJ: Rutgers University Press, 2014), xv], "Anyone who has ever tried to construct a graceful sentence around soldiers, marines, sailors, airmen, reservists, National Guard, and Coast Guard of both genders will understand this as a purely practical decision."

15 Joseph Campbell, *The Hero with a Thousand Faces*, 2nd ed. (Princeton, NJ: Princeton University Press, 1968), 30–40.

16 The soldier, as defender of the nation, glorifies patriarchy as male heroics in the service of warfare and empire, notes Christian Fuchs, "Authoritarian Capitalism, Authoritarian Movements and Authoritarian Communication," *Media, Culture and Society* 40, no. 5 (2018): 784.

17 Barbara Ehrenreich, *Blood Rites: Origins and History of the Passions of War* (New York: Henry Holt and Company, 1997), 17, 187, 198.

18 Kelly Denton-Borhaug, *U.S. War-Culture, Sacrifice and Salvation* (Oakville, CT: Equinox, 2011), 218, 229.

19 For a critical perspective on how national self-deception about America's way of war and militarization is exposed in the morally wounded veteran and how that exposure reveals the need to desacralize violence and war culture, see Kelly Denton-Barhung, *And Then Your Soul Is Gone: Moral Injury and U.S. War Culture* (Oakville, CT: Equinox, 2021).

20 Chris Hedges, "War Is a Sin," *Truthdig*, June 1, 2009, http://www.truthdig.com/report/item/20090601_war_is_sin. The violence of war has been equated in popular culture with entertainment. Roger Stahl [*Militainment, Inc.: War, Media, and Popular Culture* (New York: Routledge, 2010), 3–4, 6] calls this phenomenon "militainment," which he defines as "state violence translated into an object of pleasurable consumption [made] directly relevant to the citizen's current political life." Militainment integrates the experience of war with entertainment genres, crafting citizens into imperialist subjects by inviting them to "play the war."

21 Robert L. Ivie and Oscar Giner, *Hunt the Devil: A Demonology of US War Culture* (Tuscaloosa, AL: University of Alabama Press, 2015); Ira Chernus, *Monsters to Destroy: The Neoconservative War on Terror and Sin* (Boulder, CO: Paradigm, 2006).

22 Alexander A. Parker, *The Allegorical Drama of Calderón* (1943; Oxford: Dolphin Book Co., 1968), 77.

23 William Arrowsmith, "Editor's Foreword," in Aeschylus, *Prometheus Bound*, trans. James Scully and C. John Herington (Oxford: University Press, 1975), ix.

24 Aeschylus, *Prometheus Bound*, 35, 40.

25 Jerry Genesio, *Veterans for Peace: The First Decade* (Falmouth, ME: Pequawket Press, 1997), 16–19.

26 Genesio, 30, 34, 46.

27 Pedro de Ribadeneyra, *Vida de Ignacio de Loyola* (1572; Madrid: Espasa-Calpe, 1967), 41.

28 Genesio, 103, 45, 248.

29 Veterans for Peace, "History," *Veterans for Peace*, http://www.veteransforpeace.org/who-we-are/history/.

30 Genesio, 15.

31 Genesio, 64, 68, 74–5.

32 Mike Ferner, *Inside the Red Zone: A Veteran for Peace Reports from Iraq* (Westport, CT: Praeger, 2006), xii.

33 Ferner, 13.

34 Ferner, 22, 43–4.

35 Ferner, 91, 145.

36 Ferner, 46, 50, 52, 54.

37 Ferner, 72, 157, 23.

38 Ferner, 60–2, 148–9.

39 Veterans for Peace, "History." The 2003 invasion under President George W. Bush's orders was preceded by the invasion of Iraq in February 1991 under President George H. W. Bush's orders to push Iraq out of Kuwait.

40 Veterans for Peace, "Working Groups," *Veterans for Peace*, http://www.veteransforpeace.org/our-work/join-working-group/.

41 Veterans for Peace, "VFP Position Statements," *Veterans for Peace*, http://www.veteransforpeace.org/our-work/position-statements/.

42 Veterans for Peace," War Crimes Times Archive," *Veterans for Peace*, http://www.veteransforpeace.org/pressroom/vfp-publications/war-crimes-times-archive/.
43 Andrew J. Bacevich, "Yes, the U.S. Can Leave Afghanistan," *Veterans for Peace*, October 25, 2015, http://www.veteransforpeace.org/pressroom/news/2015/10/24/yes-us-can-leave-afghanistan.
44 Veterans for Peace, "Veterans for Peace at Home, Peace Abroad," *Veterans for Peace*, 2014, http://www.veteransforpeace.org/our-work/position-statements/veterans-peace-peace-home-peace-abroad/.
45 Veterans for Peace, "Peace at Home, Peace Abroad," *Peace in Our Times* 1, no. 1: 1, http://vfppeaceinourtimes.blogspot.com/2015_01_01_archive.html.
46 Iraq Veterans Against the War, "Founding of IVAW," *Iraq Veterans Against the War*, http://www.ivaw.org/founding-ivaw.
47 Nan Levinson, *War Is Not a Game: The New Antiwar Soldiers and the Movement They Built* (New Brunswick, NJ: Rutgers University Press, 2014), 121–2.
48 Levinson, 223.
49 Levinson, 125.
50 Edgar Lee Masters, "Harry Wilmans," in *Spoon River Anthology* (1915, 1916, 1942, 1944; New York: Macmillan Publishing, 1978), 210–11. This mythic vision of Philoctetes speaking for wounded soldiers in all wars is the original work of Oscar Giner.
51 Iraq Veterans Against the War, "Winter Soldier," http://www.ivaw.org/wintersoldier. The Winter Soldier event (held in Silver Spring, Maryland) ran from March 13 to March 16, 2008. Over 500 veterans attended the gathering in which 100 veterans testified, 7–8 per panel. Most who testified were white, young, and male. Seventy-five media outlets registered to attend. It was covered outside the U.S. in Great Britain, Slovenia, Iran, Japan, Australia, and elsewhere. Fox, CBS, AP, MTV, and Reuters set up cameras, and NPR and "Democracy Now!" conducted interviews with veterans who testified. In addition to coverage by the progressive press, reports were carried in mainstream outlets such as *Time*, the *Washington Post*, *Newsday*, *Boston Globe*, *Buffalo News*, and the *Christian Science Monitor*. It was mentioned by the *International Herald Tribune*, ignored by the *New York Times*, and covered by *Stars and Stripes* and *Military Times* (Levinson, 226–8). Overall, actual coverage in the U.S. by the corporate media was sparse (*Fairness and Accuracy in Reporting*, "Why are Winter Soldiers Not News?" March 19, 2008, http://fair.org/take-action/action-alerts/why-are-winter-soldiers-not-news/.
52 Araron Glantz, *Winter Soldier, Iraq and Afghanistan: Eyewitness Accounts of the Occupation* (Chicago, IL: Haymarket Books, 2008), 6–7.
53 Glantz, 7. On this point of intersectionality regarding continuing developments in the Veterans for Peace project, see Michael A. Messner, *Unconventional Combat: Intersectional Action in the Veterans' Peace Movement* (New York: Oxford University Press, 2021).
54 Levinson, 226, 243–5.
55 Iraq Veterans Against the War, "Why We Are Against the Wars," *Iraq Veterans Against the War*, http://www.ivaw.org/why-we-are-against-wars.
56 Iraq Veterans Against the War, "Mission, Values, and Vision," *Iraq Veterans Against the War*, http://www.ivaw.org/mission-values-and-vision.
57 Paul Chappell, *Will War Ever End?* (Weston, CT: Ashoka Books, 2009), 61, 15.

58 Benjamin Lee, Personal communication to Oscar Giner, 2015.
59 Paul Chappell, *Peaceful Revolution* (Westport, CT: Easton Studio Press, 2012), xiii, 41.
60 Chappell, *Peaceful Revolution*, 196, 14.
61 Chappell, *Peaceful Revolution*, 22, 34, 43, 45.
62 Peter Brock, "Gandhi's Nonviolence and His War Service," *Peace & Change* 7, no. 1–2 (1981): 72; Chappell, *Peaceful Revolution*, 40.
63 Chappell, *Peaceful Revolution*, 45–6.
64 Paul Chappell, *The Art of Waging Peace* (Westport, CT: Prospecta Press, 2013), 279.
65 William J. Hynes and William G. Doty, eds., *Mythical Trickster Figures: Contours, Contexts, and Criticisms* (Tuscaloosa, AL: University of Alabama Press, 1993), 4.
66 Kenneth Burke, *Permanence and Change*, 3rd ed. (Berkeley, CA: University of California Press, 1984), 69.
67 Kenneth Burke, *A Rhetoric of Motives* (1950; Berkeley: University of California Press, 1969), 18; James P. Zappen, "Kenneth Burke on Dialectical-Rhetorical Transcendence," *Philosophy and Rhetoric* 42, no. 3 (2009): 290–5.
68 Kenneth Burke, *Permanence and Change*, 108.
69 Stephen H. Daniel, *Myth and Modern Philosophy* (Philadelphia: Temple University Press, 1990), 129.
70 Kenneth Burke, *A Grammar of Motives* (1945; Berkeley: University of California Press, 1969), 504, 512.

· 4 ·

ABRAHAM'S ANGELS

> Angel guides and gifts like Saint Raphael,
> defends and avoids like Saint Michael, and
> warns like Saint Gabriel.
>
> García Lorca, "Theory and Play of *Duende*"[1]

According to Jorge Luis Borges, "primitive angels were stars." In the Book of Job, the Lord speaks out from the whirlwind about the genesis of creation, "When the morning stars sang together, and all the sons of God shouted for joy." The angel that visited the shepherds in the Gospel of Luke was accompanied by a "multitude of the heavenly host" (much like the flock of stars in the heavens). The angel that visited Joseph in the Gospel of Matthew is the same one that guided the Wise Men to Bethlehem: "We have seen his star in the east, and are come to worship him." Joseph's angel appeared in *dreams*—in that world of vision and imaginative truth that we visit nightly. "Arise, and be not afraid" is the angel's trumpet call: believe without evidence, leave what you must behind, and follow an unchartered path. Yet the wanderer is never left without guidance on the journey (Job 38:7; Luke 2:13; Matt. 1:20, 2:2, 17.7).[2]

Angel is evidence of poetry; its forms are a sign of magic. Federico García Lorca explains his own whimsical, surrealist concept of Angel:

> The angel dazzles, but flies over men's heads, is above, sheds his grace, and without effort, the man realizes his work or his sympathy or his dance. The angel of the road to Damascus and the one who entered through the chinks of the balcony of Assisi ...

orders and there is no way to oppose its lights, because he flaps his steel wings in the ambiance of the foreordained.

Angel is the symbol of a new awareness—of that human capacity for enlightenment called *anagnorisis* (recognition) which was crystallized in the form of the god Apollo by classical Greece. The structure of events in Greek tragedy compels the manifestation of ancient gods:

> OEDIPUS   Apollo   Apollo
> it was Apollo, always Apollo,
> who brought each of my agonies to birth.

"The finest recognition," wrote Aristotle, "is one that happens at the same time as a *peripety* (reversal of fortune)." At this precise moment, Oedipus discovers that he has killed his father and married his mother. At this exact juncture, angels appear in Bible stories. Angel is the emblem of action.[3]

Gabriel, The Herald Archangel

Annunciation

There is no lovelier account of the function of Angel than the story of the Annunciation to Mary (Luke 1: 26–56). In visionary trance, the seventeenth-century Spanish mystic Sor María de Agreda described the shape of Gabriel as she saw him on the eve of the Annunciation:

> His face emitted resplendent rays of light, his bearing was grave and majestic, his advance measured, his motions composed, his words weighty and powerful, his whole presence displayed a pleasing, kindly gravity and more of godlike qualities than all other angels until then seen in visible form by the heavenly Mistress. He wore a diadem of exquisite splendor and his vestments glowed in various colors full of refulgent beauty. Enchased [sic] on his breast, he bore a most beautiful cross, disclosing the mystery of the Incarnation, which He had come to announce. All these circumstances were calculated to rivet the affectionate attention of the most prudent Queen.

The presence of Angel signals a disturbance; the vision is accompanied by an internal, spiritual upheaval. A brawl ensues in the "agonized womb of consciousness," an altercation between the human mortal and the immortal image, between the inherited persona and the new revelation brought by the Messenger of God. Mary is "troubled" at Gabriel's words, but she is never the obsequious maiden of Christian lore (Luke 1:29). In Botticelli's *The Annunciation* (1489–90), Gabriel kneels in front of the young virgin, who at first rejects his portentous message and God's command with her outstretched arm and hand. In the *Annunciation* of the medieval Wakefield Cycle (fifteenth century), Mary questions the Archangel:

> I slept never by man's side,
> But in maidhood would abide
> > Unshaken.
> Therefore, I know not how
> This may be, because a vow
> > I have taken.

The acceptance of the angel's message—an act of faith and of free will—clears space in the soul for a heightened consciousness. It produces a blessing and a triumph, a reconsideration of values and behavior, and a different understanding of the world and one's place in it. Immediately after the Annunciation, Mary flees to the house of her cousin Elizabeth in the hill country, where she pronounces the *Magnificat*—her canticle in praise of the Lord who blessed her: "He that is mighty hath done to me great things; and holy is his name" (Luke 1: 46–55).[4]

Her triumph is not without pain. The struggle with the angel produces an incision, creates a wound in the recesses of the soul. In his *Gypsy Ballads* (1928), García Lorca described Gabriel's nocturnal approach to an Andalusian Mary. Lorca's Gypsy Virgin exclaims:

> Saint Gabriel: I am here for you
> with three nails of joy.
> Your splendor makes jasmines bloom
> on my shining face.[5]

Jacob's Ladder

Jacob, grandson of Abraham, tricked his twin brother Esau and took away his birthright and the blessing of their father Isaac. Esau vowed to slay his brother. Jacob journeyed from the land of his father to that of his uncle Laban to escape his brother's wrath and to find a wife. On the way to Haran, he laid down at night to sleep. In a dream, he beheld "the angels of God ascending and descending" on a ladder set on earth to reach the sky. When he woke from his dream Jacob said, "This is none other but the house of God, and this is the gate of heaven." He marked his resting place with a stone and called it Bethel (Gen. 28: 10–19).

Twenty years later, Jacob returned to the land of Isaac with his sons and wives, his camels and flocks of sheep, and all his goods and servants. As he approached the land of his relatives, he sent messengers to his brother Esau to let him know of his arrival. When Jacob was told Esau was coming to meet him with 400 men, he was "greatly afraid and distressed" because of the past enmity between them (Gen. 32: 1–20).

On the eve of his fateful encounter with his brother, Jacob sent his people and their retinue across the ford Jabbok and remained alone that night. Then Jacob "wrestled a man" until the "breaking of the day." The man did not prevail against him, but he touched the hollow of Jacob's thigh and caused it to come out of joint. At dawn, the man asked to be released from their struggle. Jacob said, "I will not let thee go, except thou bless me." The man replied, "Thy name shall be called no more Jacob, but Israel; for as a prince hast thou power with God and with men, and hast prevailed." He received his yearned-for blessing from the strange man and called the place Peniel, "for I have seen God face to face, and my life is preserved." As the sun "rose upon him," Jacob "halted upon his thigh" (Gen. 32: 22–32).

It is reasonable to assume that Jacob's wrestling match occurred in a dream. The King James passage identifies the wrestler as a "man," but the wound inflicted by Angel is recognizable in Jacob's halting thigh. The nightlong struggle ends in a victory of awareness for the son of Isaac, revealing his adversary as one who displays prophetic power and wields authority to bless. The rising sun over Peniel is emblematic of the illumination and clarity that Angel brings. Jacob's name becomes Israel as a sign of divinity shed upon mortals; he will no longer be an exile, but a powerful prince.

The figure of Angel stands in-between Jacob and his God. Its blessings depend on a release, on the letting go of an old persona and the giving up of commodities acquired. Jacob sends his flocks and herds as a propitiating gift to his brother. He suffers a wound and changes his name according to the prophecy spoken by his wrestling opponent. These are characteristic of *divestiture*—a process that consists of the stripping away of old habits, shedding antiquated identities and surrendering possessions that imprison the self in preparation for a divine unveiling. Divestiture results in a nakedness, a required vulnerability in the story's protagonist before Angel is perceived in a world of shadows.

Only those who achieve a state of readiness through sedulous effort acquire a positive disposition towards the struggle. In a renowned account of one of her trances, Saint Therese of Avila ("that extraordinary producer and organizer of images and metaphors") describes the rapture of a soul which has prepared to receive the angelic vision:

> I saw in his hands a long dart of gold, and at the end of the rod there was a bit of fire. This he seemed to plunge into my heart sometimes, and reached deep inside me; and when he took it out all of me seemed to go with it, and left me burning in great love of God. The pain was so great that I moaned, and so excessive was the softness of this great pain, that you cannot wish it away, nor is the soul satisfied with anything less than God.

The apparition of Angel causes a decomposition of internal structures inherited from the past, opening consciousness to new structures of meaning. This moment is immortalized by Bernini in "The Ecstasy of Saint Teresa" (seventeenth century) at the church of Santa Maria della Vitoria in Rome.[6]

The struggle may precede the surprising apparition of Angel. In such cases, the protagonist is astonished, and the agony occurs in a dark realm. The internal struggle *creates* the angel and *compels* its manifestation in aesthetic form, as is the case with Paul on the road to Damascus. Saul is struck blind for three days after falling to the earth when "a light from heaven" surrounded him. The Voice of the Lord moves Saul to see "in a vision a man named Ananias coming in." When God's disciple places his hands on Saul, the *illumination* of Angel fills him with the Holy Spirit. Divestiture—followed by Crisis—sets up the alchemy that restores Saul's eyesight. The crisis allows the presence of Angel (or Devil) to be *sensed*, but the hero can perceive neither figure until *divestiture* has occurred, which precedes *illumination*: "There fell from his eyes as it had been scales: and he received sight forthwith." Henceforth his name will be Paul (Acts 9: 3–18).

Jekyll and Hyde

Jacob's dream of the wrestling match on the banks of Jabbok is an emblem of the constant, continuous struggle between twin polarities within us. For the Persian physician and mystic Avicenna (980–1037), the self "is composed of a reunion of a celestial Angel with a 'fallen' Angel; they are the two wings of the soul." For Christopher Marlowe (1564–93), two dialoguing angels attended the passage of Dr. Faustus from Wittenberg scholar to condemned soul:

> *Good Angel.* Faustus, repent yet, God will pity thee.
> *Evil Angel.* Thou art a spirit. God cannot pity thee. (2.3.12–13)

For Robert Louis Stevenson in the nineteenth century, "man is not truly one, but truly two." Human beings are "commingled" out of good and evil. The Jekyll/Hyde duality consists of dissenting, embodied personas existing within the same individual being. At certain times, a *crisis* develops and shakes the "prison-house" of our disposition, heightening the awareness of internal tension and threatening to cause an imbalance in "the very fortress of identity." For Jacob in Genesis, his looming encounter with Esau is such a crisis. Jacob does not see the angel until he has found grace, and Dr. Faustus cannot call the devil until he has turned his back on salvation. For Henry Jekyll, drinking his salt potion is such a divestiture. The evil countenance of Edward Hyde reflected in his bedroom's mirror runs to the surface and breaks through, like the "captives at Philippi."[7]

Better Angels

The North American mystic Thomas Merton—beat poet in Cistercian monk garb—points out where to find the living presence of Angel in our time:

> Alone in the woodshed on St. Stephen's Day [I read] some Emily Dickinson, my own flesh and blood, my own kind of quiet rebel. ... She gave herself completely to people of other ages and places who never saw her, but who could receive her gift anyway, regardless of space and time. It is like hugging an angel.

The poetry of Dickinson (1830–86) is a supreme example of receptivity to a new awareness. Form and effect of angelic apparitions are precisely drawn:

> (477)
> Your Breath—has time to straighten —
> Your Brain—to bubble cool —
> Deals One—imperial Thunderbolt —
> That scalps your naked soul—

She "*perceives abstraction* and *thinks sensation*," wrote the poet Allen Tate. "[Cotton] Mather would have burnt her for a witch."[8]

In 1855, Emily Dickinson and her family moved back to their ancestral home in Amherst, where she wrote many of her poems. She was 24 years old. Scarcely more than one half-decade later, Abraham Lincoln made his way to the platform in front of the Capitol in Washington from which he delivered the First Inaugural Address. He was 52. She was heir to the Puritan tradition of New England; he was a Son of the Prairie. Dickinson became a notorious recluse during her time; Lincoln became one of the most photographed personalities of the nineteenth century. Yet they shared commonalities that have canonized them as mythical American figures. Both derived their language from the American biblical tradition and from the plays of Shakespeare. According to one author, "biblical quotations in [Dickinson's] letters and poems far exceed references to any other source or author." She treasured her "Lexicon" (Noah Webster's dictionary, 1856 edition), and once said about the works of Shakespeare: "Why is any other book needed?"[9]

Lincoln quoted profusely from the King James Bible in his writings and speeches. He would "read and think" late into the night in the White House library, "his large leather bible beside him." He was an avid theatergoer and a shrewd student of Shakespeare:

> Some of Shakespeare's plays I have never read; while others I have gone over perhaps as frequently as any unprofessional reader. Among the latter are Lear, Richard the Third, Henry Eighth, Hamlet, and especially Macbeth. I think nothing equals Macbeth. It is wonderful. ... I think the soliloquy in Hamlet commencing "O, my offence is rank" surpasses that commencing "To be, or not to be."

Precedents for Lincoln's better angels of the First Inaugural can be found in *Hamlet*, when the young prince meets his father's ghost—"Angels and ministers of grace defend us!" (1.4.42)—and in Horatio's prayer after Hamlet's death—"And flights of angels sing thee to thy rest!" (5.2.371). Angels also make an appearance in Gratiano's lament over the dead Desdemona in *Othello*:

> I am glad thy father's dead. ...
> This sight would make him do a desperate turn,
> Yea, curse his *better angel* from his side,
> And fall to reprobation.[10] (5.2.241–6)

Upon completion of one of the final drafts of the First Inaugural, Lincoln gave reading copies of his text to his Secretary of State, William Seward. Seward suggested a final paragraph for the address that included the evocation of a blessing by a metaphorical guardian angel over the nation:

> The mystic chords which proceeding from so many battle fields and so many patriot graves pass through all the hearts and all the hearths in this broad continent of ours

will yet again harmonize in their ancient music when breathed upon by *the guardian angel of the nation*.

Lincoln transfigured Seward's prose:

> The mystic chords of memory, stretching from every battle-field, and patriot grave, to every living heart and hearthstone, all over this broad land, will yet swell the chorus of the Union, when again touched, as surely they will be, by *the better angels of our nature*.

The difference is a more imaginative rendering of the "mystic chords" which bind the nation and a deeper belief in the substance and function of angels. Lincoln's "better angels," writes Doris Kearns Goodwin, "are inherent in our nature as a people."[11]

For both, Dickinson in white and Lincoln in rumpled black and stovepipe hat, angels are structures of the soul perceived as divine beings. Agents of the self, they are reflective mirrors to be conjured or ignored—much like the Devil—as the occasion warrants.

Raphael, the Healing Archangel

The Archangel of Temperance is Raphael, who stands between the deep waters of the self and the shores of our persona. This is the Angel who accompanied the son of Tobit in his journey, and who stood on the banks of the river Tigris as Tobias grabbed the fish for the salve that restored his father's eyesight. This same Archangel chained the Devil in far regions and cleansed the world from his influence. Raphael embodies the equilibrium that promises survival after trials. He goes in and out before the glory of God, transforms wounded warriors into wounded healers, and helps to bury the dead.

Gethsemane

In February 1864, F.B. Carpenter was called to the White House to produce a commemorative painting of the reading of the Emancipation Proclamation. Knowing the President's fondness for Shakespeare, Carpenter relayed that the legendary American tragedian Edwin Booth would play an engagement at Grover's Theatre in Washington. Lincoln had never seen Booth act Hamlet, and proposed attending his performance of the play, even though "it matters not to me ... whether Shakespeare be well or ill acted—with him the thought suffices." The news "awakened" a train of thought in Lincoln that drove him to recite King Claudius' soliloquy from memory in *Hamlet*. Lincoln believed that Claudius' speech after the play-within-the-play called *The Murder of Gonzago* (re-written as "The Mousetrap") to be "one of the finest touches of nature in the world."[12]

Weighed down by guilt, defiled by incest and adultery, the King of Denmark cannot repent or pray for mercy:

> Oh, wretched state! O bosom black as death!
> Oh, limed soul that struggling to be free
> Art more engaged! Help angels!—Make assay:
> Bow stubborn knees, and heart with strings of steel.
> Be soft as sinews of the new-born babe. (3.3.67–71)

The scene is a reverse echo of Christ's agony in Gethsemane on the night before the Crucifixion. Jesus prays for the chalice of his trial to pass from him; immediately, an angel from heaven appears, "strengthening him" (Luke: 22:43). Claudius cannot see his angel because only the shedding of "those effects for which I did the murder" can compel the apparitions of the messenger of God (3.3.54). The much-quoted "better angels of our nature" of the First Inaugural is an echo of his anguished lament on his knees: "Help, angels!—Make assay."[13]

One may surmise in reading *Hamlet* that Lincoln saw himself as the guilty creature "struck ... to the soul" by the "very cunning of the scene" (2.2.543–4). Throughout the early years of the fratricidal war that he unleashed upon the nation, he scarcely mentioned the better angels he invoked in 1861. Lincoln came to see the war as a purgatory to which the country was condemned because of the sin of slavery. The War was penance, and salvation would be gained only through repentance, which would take the form of ridding the country of the ghastly institution:

> If God wills that [the war] continue, until all the wealth piled by the bond-man's two hundred and 50 years of unrequited toil shall be sunk, and until every drop of blood drawn with the lash, shall be paid by another drawn with the sword. ... [S]o still it must be said "the judgments of the Lord, are true and righteous altogether."

For the blessings of Angel to become manifest, North and South would need to shed their burden like Bunyan's Pilgrim—into the mouth of the open sepulcher at the foot of the Cross. The gesture would compel the apparition of angels and their bounty. But Claudius' prayer fails:

> Try what repentance can. What can it not?
> Yet what can it when one cannot repent? (3.3.65–6)

Gore Vidal's historical novel *Lincoln* proposes a terrifying finale to Lincoln's story: "In some mysterious fashion, [he] had willed his own murder as a form of atonement for the great and terrible thing that he had done by giving so bloody and absolute a rebirth to his nation."[14]

Love's Idol Lost

On February 20, 1862, 11-year-old William Wallace, son of Abraham Lincoln, died of typhoid fever in the White House. Elizabeth Keckley, a former slave who was dressmaker to Mary Todd Lincoln, described Lincoln's grief at the deathbed of his son: "Great sobs choked his utterance. He buried his head in his hands, and his tall frame was convulsed with emotion. … —genius and greatness weeping over love's idol lost." One day, in the spring of 1862, while reading from a volume of Shakespeare, Lincoln called out to one of his staff officers: "I want to read you a passage in *Hamlet*!" He read aloud from *Hamlet*, *Macbeth*, and also recited Constance's plaintive lament from *King John* about the capture by English forces of her young son Arthur (12 years old, disputed heir to the throne of England). Constance explains that her mourning keeps her close to her imprisoned child:

> Grief fills the room up of my absent child,
> Lies in his bed, walks up and down with me,
> Puts on his pretty looks, repeats his words,
> Remembers me of all his gracious parts,
> Stuffs out his vacant garments with his form;
> Then have I reason to be fond of grief! (3.3.93–8)

Lincoln questioned his aide: "Colonel, did you ever dream of a lost friend, and feel that you were holding a sweet communion with that friend, and yet have a sad consciousness that it was not a reality?" He added, "Just so I dream of my boy Willie."[15]

"The pestilence that is the usual accompaniment of war" ravaged the children of Civil War combatants during the conflict. Neither Federal nor Confederate was spared as an Exterminating Angel of happenstance and disease conducted its own massacre of the innocents. Tecumseh Sherman lost his nine-year-old son, who "contracted" typhoid fever on a visit to his father's military camp. Southern General James Longstreet lost two young boys to scarlet fever when his family moved to Richmond. Five-year-old Joseph Davis, son of Jefferson and Varina Davis, perished from a fall from the porch of the executive mansion in Richmond. In 1864, in refugee camps near Nashville, "the mortality rate among women and children was fearful." It was the price both slaveholders and abolitionists paid for their commitment to country and to their ideals—the reward all men receive when they sacrifice their offspring to what James Joyce called "my home, my fatherland or my church."[16]

The loss of Willie and Abraham Lincoln's deep affection for the Bible may have brought to his attention the familiar story of Abraham and Isaac from the Book of Genesis. The tale is briefly told in King James: the Voice of God orders Abraham to take Isaac to a mountain in the Land of Moriah and sacrifice him as a burnt offering. On the third day of travel, Abraham "lifted up his eyes" and saw the mountain from afar. He laid the wood for the pyre on Isaac's back, and with a firebrand in one hand and a knife in the other, he walked up the mountain with his son. The text records only a single utterance by Isaac: "Behold the fire and the wood: but where is the lamb for a burnt offering?" To which his father replied, "My son, God will provide himself a lamb." Abraham built an altar, prepared the wood, and bound Isaac on the altar. He raised the sacrificial knife to kill his son, but the Angel of the Lord called out to him: "Lay not thine hand upon the lad." Abraham "lifted up his eyes" again and saw a ram ensnared in a thicket. He caught the ram and offered it "in the stead of his son." Abraham called this place of sacrifice "Je-hó-vah-jí-reh" ("In the mount of the Lord it shall be seen," Gen. 22: 1–14).

Soren Kierkegaard's "Dialectical Lyric" *Fear and Trembling* is dedicated to the story of Abraham and Isaac. Kierkegaard makes a distinction between two types of dramatic characters: (1) the "tragic "hero," who "renounces himself in order to express the universal"; and (2) the "knight of faith," who "renounces the universal in order to be the particular." An example of the first is Agamemnon in Euripides' *Iphigeneia at Aulis*. The Greek general bows to the demands of the goddess Artemis and the exigencies of the Achaian fleet by promising to sacrifice his young daughter. Agamemnon "sacrifices himself and everything he has for the universal; ... he is the beloved son of ethics." An example of the second is Abraham, who "determines his relation to the universal through his relation to the absolute." When God compels Abraham to sacrifice Isaac, the patriarch becomes an "emigrant from the sphere of the universal."[17]

Both the tragic hero and the knight of faith must resign their claims to Iphigeneia and Isaac, respectively. Agamemnon addresses his young daughter: "It is Greece compels me/to sacrifice you, whatever I wish" (1706–8). In Abraham's case, resignation occurs during his journey to the land of Moriah. Kierkegaard writes that Abraham says to himself on his way up to the hill, "It won't happen, or if it does the Lord will give me a new Isaac on the strength of the absurd." As he prepares to kill his son, a great silence descends upon the scene. In "distress and anguish," Abraham cannot speak: "Silence is both [divine and demonic]. It is the demon's lure, and the more silent one keeps the more terrible the demon becomes; but silence is also divinity's communion with the individual." At this point, when all inherited frames of references crumble, the Angel appears.[18]

With this in mind, we can propose an interpretive moral for the myth of Abraham and Isaac that informs, but is unacknowledged, by the King James narrative. It lies submerged not only in the Bible story, but also in subsequent medieval and contemporary versions of the tale.

Caliban's Island

In the Puerto Rican theater tradition in Spanish, playwright René Marqués (1919–79) holds the same stature as that of Eugene O'Neill in the U.S.—foremost among equals. In 1969, Marqués published an allegory of the Vietnam War based on the story of Abraham and Isaac: *Sacrificio en el Monte Moriah* [*Sacrifice on Mount Moriah*]. As inspiration for the play, Marqués credited a conversation with his son, Raúl, about the "concept of anguish" in the works of Kierkegaard. The published version of *Sacrificio* contained an introductory overview of Marqués' play; "Preliminary Notes" by the author on the biblical legend; a "Minimal Bibliography"; the text of the play in "fourteen cinematographic scenes"; and an appendix—including floor plans for the stage design—with instructions from the author on how to produce the play. The play was framed by bookend dedications to two young Puerto Ricans who opposed the war in Far East Asia. Marqués penned the first dedication for his son, who at the time was incarcerated for refusing induction into the U.S. Army:

> For ... my firstborn, who has refused, following the dictates of his conscience, to join the army through the Obligatory Military Service law and whom I would never be willing to sacrifice on the altar of a bloody and bellicose entity, I dedicate, with admiration as a Puerto Rican and a father's deep love and pride, *Sacrificio en el Monte Moriah*.
>
> René Marqués

The second was a brief obituary for a young friend, Rafael Varona, who was killed in North Vietnam by a U.S. bombing raid while he studied in Hanoi as part of a visiting group of young Latin American observers. The emotional dedications by Marqués were a protest against an unjust war, and a powerful affirmation of Puerto Rican identity against the colonial power that enslaved the island and threatened its native character.[19]

Elizabethan poets, playwrights, and historians employed the practice of *application* (the selection of a story from the past "intending the application of it to [their] time") to either perceive the world through the prism of aesthetic distance or to conceal, through the assumption of a historical mask, the critique of a contemporary political regime. *Sacrificio en el Monte Moriah* was conceived as such an allegorical play.[20]

In 1898, during the final days of the Spanish American War, the U.S. invaded the island of Puerto Rico to establish an imperial presence in the Caribbean. With permanent naval bases in Cuba and Puerto Rico, the U.S. would secure the historical gateway to the Americas. In 1917, Congress granted U.S. citizenship to all Puerto Ricans. Today, the political relationship between the U.S. and Puerto Rico most closely resembles the sovereignty arrangements between the U.S. and Native American nations. The Commonwealth of Puerto Rico is an Indian reservation without the right to vote in presidential elections. In 1960, writing a scathing critique of over half a century of Puerto Rican political, economic, and cultural submission to the U.S., René Marqués argued:

> We are docile. If we were not, Puerto Rico would have obtained its national sovereignty in the 19th century. ... Puerto Ricans can be antisocial, defiant, non-conformist occasionally and even heroic as individuals in some cases, but we are certainly docile as a people.

From the first Taíno insurrection by Agueybaná el Bravo [the Brave] in 1511; to the repulsion of repeated British and Danish invasions during the Spanish colony; to the slave rebellions of the nineteenth century; to the "Grito de Lares" insurrection against Spanish rule in 1865; to the Puerto Rican participation in the Cuban War of Independence in 1895; in all conflicts Puerto Ricans have demonstrated the fighting spirit that animated the legendary "Borinqueneers" during the Korean War. The Puerto Rican armed struggle for independence brought about the Ponce Massacre (1937), the Nationalist Revolt (1950), the Blair House attack on Harry Truman's life (1950), the armed assault on the U.S. Congress (1956), and more recently, the attacks in the U.S. mainland and Puerto Rico by the *Macheteros* and other nationalist groups. Imagine conceiving Sitting Bull, Crazy Horse, and Geronimo as "peaceful"; picture the Cheyenne and Lakota at Little Bighorn, the proud Navajo, or the ferocious Apache as "docile" because their nations have not yet gained independence![21]

The Docile Puerto Rican

In Marqués' drama of the Abraham and Isaac story, Abraham is a fiercely orthodox executioner of God's orders. There are no angelic apparitions in the play, only the brief advent of a Young Stranger dressed in white, who announces the destruction of Sodom and Gomorrah. The Patriarch chooses to believe that his guest is a divine messenger. Abraham does not negotiate for the survival of the doomed cities; he merely asks the Stranger to spare Lot and his family.

Sara is not a Hebrew, but a foreigner who is a Sumerian princess. She bitterly resents Abraham's infertility and his inability to protect the Land of Canaan from imperial invasions. Because Abraham delivers her as a concubine to both the Egyptian Pharaoh and Abimelech of Gerar, Sara vows enmity against the god that the Patriarch follows blindly.

On top of Mount Moriah, Isaac clamors for his mother: "Set me free, father. Don't make me a victim to the sacrifice. Mother! Mother!" Over the sacrificial pyre, *"transfigured into a wild beast,"* Abraham draws the ritual knife and prays to Yahweh. Now hesitating, with knife drawn over the bound Isaac (like Hamlet with sword drawn over the kneeling Claudius) Abraham pauses during his oration:

> ABRAHAM. (Arrested in murderous impulse, lost in anguish and confusion.)
> Lord, if my name is Abraham how can I be "father of multitudes" if I kill my legitimate heir? ... (*Pause. In supreme anguish.*) Speak to me! Look at the anguish in my heart. (*Pause.*) I cannot hear your voice. How to interpret the absence of your divine voice? (*Brief pause.*) Your silence then is my command.

In "distress and anguish," Abraham enters the silence of which Kierkegaard writes: "Abraham *cannot speak*. What would explain everything, that it is a trial ... is something he cannot say (i.e., in a way that can be understood)."[22]

The Silence

The Burkean frame of reference (which includes both frames of acceptance and frames of rejection) has collapsed. A brief pause endures an eternity, space is present all at once, and the necessity of choice without context becomes imperative. Silence awakens latent inclinations in the soul of the Patriarch and compels an original choice provoking form, which is a prophetic crystallization that incites action—like the dagger in Macbeth's fatal vision before the murder of Duncan. Abraham responds by retreating from the void that surrounds him. He falls back to the old-world vision—now empty of meaning—which brought him to this predicament. Possessed by the dragon, he chooses to obey his outdated God and destroy the child who is the promised seed of his future nation. His choice is an example of a Burkean event in which "an imaginative possibility ... is bureaucratized."[23]

The manifestation of Angel in *Monte Moriah* is only the masquerading Sara, who wears a white, hooded robe in imitation of the garment worn by the Young Stranger in an earlier scene. She chased after Abraham and Isaac and now performs a *deus ex machina* pageant of apparition. Standing on a promontory while Abraham is silent, Sara tricks him into believing she is a Messenger of God: "Here I am before you, Abraham, as an Angel from Yahweh. 'Do not extend your hand over the boy, do nothing to him, because now I know you fear Yahweh'." Abraham concludes that Sara's intervention is that of an angelic being. While her husband lays trembling on the ground, she hides Isaac in the folds of her robe, and they flee the scene. But not before Isaac stops and turns back to regard his father: "Something very great has died within me. ... My faith, Mother, my faith."[24]

In the catalog of Abraham and Isaac plays, *Sacrificio en el Monte Moriah* is unique in that Isaac opposes Yahweh's edict and rebels against it. At a celebration of his coming of age (years after the attempted sacrifice), Isaac rejects Abraham's devotion to Yahweh and accuses Sara of complicity in his father's submission to foreigners:

> I want another god if I am to have one. One of love and peace, of liberty and generosity. One that understands the miseries of humanity. One that is not a despot. One that never asks for human sacrifices to satisfy his thirst for power and vengeance.

Under the threat of his father's sacrificial knife, Isaac also experienced silence. In silence came the undoing of his faith; from silence he conjured up the vision of a new God. Sara attempts to break—unsuccessfully—from her own subservience to Abraham's rule through political assassination. In the final scene she stabs Abraham in the heart and stands over Abraham's corpse, like Clytemnestra over the corpse of Agamemnon, cawing in defiance against Yahweh: "Send me to the abyss of shadows. You know well that I have tried, against your will, to free the people you enslaved by calling them yours."[25]

The Satan

Abraham's Angel, according to Elaine Pagels, was what ancient Hebrew storytellers called the *satan*—a messenger "not necessarily evil, much less opposed to God," but rather "one of God's obedient servants." The *satan* accounts for "unexpected obstacles or reversals of fortune," and with God's license, can oppose directions of human activity:

> God sends him, like the angel of death, to perform a specific task, although one that human beings may not appreciate. ... The *satan* may simply have been sent by the Lord to protect a person from worse harm.

Michelangelo da Caravaggio's (1571–1610) *The Sacrifice of Isaac* (1603) illustrates this function of the *satan*. When Abraham is about to kill Isaac, the angel/*satan* does not simply announce God's reversal of his edict; he grabs Abraham by the arm preventing Isaac's beheading and gazes sternly at the Patriarch: "What wouldst thou do, old man?"[26]

From immeasurable silence, there is transmutation to a New Order. In the Bible story, the apparition of Angel is a consequence of the destruction of the symbolic order of Abraham's world. Upon hearing—or more precisely, calling upon his own agency to "create"—the Voice of Angel out of silence, Abraham "*lifted up his eyes*" and saw the wrong he would commit. At that moment, he *chooses to reject the nature of his God and to transform his command.* After the angelic vision, Abraham looked and *saw* (a second act of "creative" imagination) "a ram caught in a thicket by his horns." The moral of the story is clear: when tasked by the cruelty and injustice of your symbolic system, *change your God* (Gen. 22: 13).

The spiritual transcendence occurs in the bosom of Isaac. He switches his allegiance from his father's "bloody and bellicose entity" to a god of "love and peace, kindness and liberty." The apparition of Angel is not a form of comic corrective; it is a sign of altered meaning. From then on, the ultimate symbol in a decrepit mystic hierarchy—the outdated Old Testament God—perishes in the dust.[27]

The Wall

René Marqués' play is an allegory that is referential to the colonial subjection of Puerto Rico and to the military conscription of its young citizens by the U.S. during the Vietnam war. In Washington D.C., where another Abraham once sacrificed the youth of the nation to free the slaves, we have consecrated a great monument to the blame and shame of our war folly. It was constructed by the grief of fathers and mothers who chose duty to flag, country, profits, ideals, over filial obligation to sons and daughters. It tells a story as old as that of the young Antigone, who demanded burial rites for her fallen brother from Old King Kreon, who was made inflexible by his wrath and his devotion to the state.

Designed by Maya Lin, a daughter of Chinese immigrants and a member of the generation that followed the Vietnam War, the Vietnam Veterans Memorial was inspired by Yale University's Memorial Hall. The original memorial walls were dedicated in 1915 to "the men of Yale who gave their lives in the Civil War." Uniquely, the names of both Union and Confederate soldiers are inscribed on the corridor's walls. As an undergraduate, Lin observed the etchings on the walls and observed "the sense of the power of a name." She intended to create a space "where the simple meeting of earth, sky and remembered names contains messages for all."[28]

The Wall is best visited when there are no crowds. You commune with the dead at night, with only footlights to light your path and the light of stars to light the names of the dead.

> Thompson
> Nakayama
> Lozada
> Covington
> Johnson
> Charlie Berry

A phantom legion who fought and died responds to an Asian voice that calls: "In war, no one wins or loses."

Facing Death on the Wall, excuses vanish—so great is the burden of regrets:

> Died for a way of life?
> "A curse on your life and lifestyle."
> For democracy? Our freedom?

"Die for your own damn freedom. I'll die for mine."

The Wall is an evocation of ancestors, of fathers demanding—like Maya priests offering up young victims as human sacrifices to the Sun—and sons consenting to zealotry in a worthless conflict.[29]

(Raphael's arresting hand intervenes.) *There is a way out of madness.*

In 1971, during a week of protests by the Vietnam Veterans Against the War in Washington D.C., several hundred veterans threw the medals they had received for service in Vietnam over a fence of wood and wire, erected before the Capitol to prevent protesters from reaching Congress—wilted flowers flung at a grave site. One by one, the vets stepped up to a microphone and rejected their past, renounced their heritage, and recanted their engagement in the war: *I don't want these fucking medals, man!*

John Musgrave (deployed in '67) served 11 months in Vietnam. He chronicles his encounter with his father after coming home from the VVAW demonstrations:

> When I got home…
> my dad's pissed off
> 'cause … he's a true
> believer, you know?
> He was already receiving threats
> because I'd thrown away *their* medals.
> And that pissed my dad off. …
> And he said, "Son, don't worry.
> Those were your medals.
> You paid for 'em
> you can do anything you want with 'em.
> They wanna jack with us,
> they'll face us both."

In the Book of Genesis, once Abraham entered the silence, he did not speak to the Angel that stopped him and did not ask forgiveness from his son. But now we know what he said to Isaac before offering the ram in his stead: "We'll take 'em on the driveway. You know?"[30]

Michael, the Exterminating Angel

Michael the Archangel argued with the Devil over the body of Moses and fought against the Dragon and his Legion (Jude 1:9 and Rev. 12:7–9). Over the river Tiber in Rome, a causeway of angel statues bridges Vatican City with Castel Sant'Angelo. On top of the fortress stands a bronze statue of Michael sheathing his sword, signaling the end of battle. During the plague of 590, the Archangel and his host fended off a legion of evil spirits. Michael was one of the saints (along with Catherine of Alexandria and Margaret of Antioch) who spoke to and inspired Joan of Arc. He is the spiritual warrior invoked by Irish rebels, and the patron saint of U.S. Marines. His path can be traced through Luis Buñuel's surrealist classic *The Exterminating Angel* (1962).

Three Angels

In the desert, at the worst time of day, heat seeps through your pores, dries up the organs of the body and distempers the rational mind, giving way to mirages. While Abraham sat in front of his tent, the Lord appeared to him in the form of Three Men. (Marc Chagall visualized these figures as angels in his painting *Abraham et les trois Anges* [and the three Angels]). Abraham welcomed his visitors, invited them to rest under the shade of a tree and gave them bread, butter, milk, and meat from a tender calf to eat. He stood by the tree while the Voice of the Lord prophesied that Sarah, even in her old age, would give birth to a son. The destruction of Sodom and Gomorrah had been ordained because their sin was grievous. Two of the Men stood up, turned their faces, and left in the direction of Sodom. In their wake, Abraham engaged in negotiation with the remaining Angel of the Lord. The Spanish Golden Age poet and playwright Sor Juana Inés de la Cruz (born and died in New Spain/Mexico, 1648–95) believed that Abraham's conversation with the Lord (Gen. 18: 23–33) was constructed along geometrical lines, reflecting divine musical patterns:

> Without being expert in Music, how might one understand those musical intervals … that occur in … Abraham's petitions to God on behalf of the Cities, beseeching God to spare them if there were found fifty righteous people within?

The communication between angels and mortals is rhythmic and ritualistic. The language of angels is musical, like Ariel's songs in Shakespeare's *The Tempest*. The oracle should be understood as poetic discourse: allusive rather than explicit, prophetic instead of sententious.[31]

Abraham persuades the deity to think like him by transforming God rhetorically. The content of Abraham's argument haunts us to this day:

1. A pressing query: "Wilt thou ... destroy the righteous with the wicked?"
2. A rebuke: "That be far from thee to do after this manner, to slay the righteous with the wicked."
3. A gradual reduction of expectations by diminishing the number of righteous inhabitants required for salvation: "Peradventure there shall lack five of the fifty righteous: wilt thou destroy all the city for lack of five?" (Or forty, thirty, etc.)
4. Finally, a categorical judgment: "Shall not the Judge of all the earth do right?"

The dialogue is a continuous challenge to God's decree of extinction. It generates a measured, systematic humanization of the deity, calling upon God's presumed virtues of perspective, mercy, justice, and fair play. Just like Prospero before Ariel, the Old Testament God is moved to a degree of compassion through the skilled treatment of Abraham:

> Ariel. If you now beheld them, your affections
>   Would become tender.
> Prospero. Dost thou think so, spirit?
> Ariel. Mine would, sir, were I human. (5.1.18–20)

Angelic revelations operate to provoke ethical, ideal, emotional, or physical reactions in human beings. But also in each case, the human agent that receives the angelic message speaks back a discourse from the heart, which operates upon the spirit symbol:

1. Gabriel's Annunciation brings the revelation of a New Order to Mary; Mary bestows the Word Made Flesh upon Angel.
2. Yahweh demands the human sacrifice of Isaac, but Abraham changes his god, and makes the scapegoat ram a burnt offering acceptable to Yahweh.
3. Abraham's Three Angels announce the destruction of Sodom and Gomorrah; in turn, Abraham persuades the Lord to give up the annihilation of the cities for the sake of 10 righteous men.

The resulting divine message blends Abraham's mortality with the mystery and spirituality of Angel, thus creating the philosopher's stone on the far shore of the sea of transcendence: *It is not the presence of the wicked that matters, but the absence of the righteous what makes cities extinct.*

Hiroshima Shadows

From here on the story moves swiftly, as if constructed according to the classical unities. The Exterminating Angels enter Sodom at sundown and warn Lot and his family to leave the city, because "the Lord hath sent us to destroy it" (Gen. 19:13). In the morning, the angels take Lot, his wife and daughters by their hands and put them outside the city. "Then the Lord rained upon Sodom and upon Gomorrah brimstone and fire from the Lord out of heaven" (Gen. 19:24). The day of the destruction of the cities, Abraham woke early in the morning and saw a pillar of smoke rise from the plain "as the smoke of a furnace" (Gen 19:28). The denouement of Sodom and Gomorrah may be approximated by recalling the bombing of Hiroshima. No one remembered hearing a noise from a bomb. Across the sky, everything flashed white, like "a sheet of the sun." The clouds of dust, the flames and the ensuing twilight made the inhabitants believe that a star had fallen to the earth. "Bursts of hot air and showers of cinders" made it impossible to stand. Lot's wife may have turned to see "a rising atomic mushroom cloud." She was vaporized—"consumed" according to King James—and turned into a pillar of salt. Then Lot went to live in a mountain cave with his two daughters.[32]

John Huston's *The Bible: In the Beginning* (1966) was conceived as the first of a series of films (never completed) on the first 26 books of the Bible. The second half of the film is dedicated to the story of Abraham. On the road to Mount Moriah, Abraham and Isaac pass through a landscape in ruins—as if a nuclear device had flashed above it. They observe petrified human remains, animal figures, and broken columns:

> ABRAHAM: The city of Sodom. ... [The Lord] overthrew these cities, and all the plain, and all the inhabitants of the cities, and that which grew upon the face of the ground.
> ISAAC: All the inhabitants?

The visitation to the ruins of Sodom reveals the psychological context for Abraham's actions and highlights the tension that torments the Patriarch: to please his God, he must sacrifice his son; if he does not sacrifice his son, a wrathful God will break his covenant and destroy his progeny. The scene also explains Isaac's compliance: he will consent to the sacrifice for the sake of his people, like Iphigeneia in Euripides' play. Huston makes palpable the urgency of the decision by associating visually Sodom in ruins with modern cities devastated by wars.[33]

The choice that Abraham contemplates is one that we have wrestled with in our time. Sacrifice your children or your country will be ravaged by fire and brimstone; send your offspring to Iraq or your people will perish like the denizens of Sodom and Gomorrah. In the aftermath of 9/11, Condoleezza Rice, Secretary of State in the George W. Bush administration, put the choice very effectively when she urged the nation to invade Iraq or suffer a nuclear explosion: "We don't want the smoking gun to be a mushroom cloud." The Exterminating Angels make Genesis come alive before the mind's eye. But a peace-waging nation would recognize this binary choice as a fallacy and would have chosen the way of Abraham: recant the bellicose deity, summon the angel at the threshold of revelation, and follow your guide to the brambles where the ram is caught by the horns.[34]

Conclusions: Angelary

One of the main lessons of the Abraham stories is that humans are conversant with angels. Angels are much more than mere abstractions; they are also ideas that become *humanized* through our interactions. Calderón de la Barca described such distilled images as *imagined concepts*—ideas that partake of human form. These interactions with angels are musical, as befit conversations with beings that are essentially aesthetic. In *The Wasteland*, T. S. Eliot paints a picture of how we receive the songs of angels:

> Musing upon the king my brother's wreck
> And on the king my father's death before him …
> "This music crept by me upon the waters."

Eliot is preceded by Ferdinand in Shakespeare's *Tempest*:

> Allaying both their fury and my passion
> With its sweet air. Thence I have followed it,
> Or it hath drawn me rather. (1.2.392–5)

Like Ariel's songs, angelic messages flow to us from the heavenly spheres or erupt from the depths of the sea.[35]

In our wretched days, we are forced to understand Abraham's angels as metaphors or (at worst) as disembodied concepts without aesthetic mediation. To grasp an angel's message, we must accept vision as an aesthetic symbol. We must acknowledge not only what is intelligible, but also what is unfathomable and will only reveal itself in time. To explain away the angel is to limit its complexity and reduce its apparition to a mere eventuality. We should regard angels as classical Greece once regarded heroes. Writing about the final scene of Euripides' *Alcestis*, William Arrowsmith explains:

> [We] must make an effort to ... understand how events happen in mythical time, uniquely and forever, and that "hero" is the name for real *presence*, venerable and abiding, that survives the death of the body.

You do not patronize Angel's manifestations—you identify them and honor them. You do not paraphrase the message by ignoring artistic form; you understand that "content is what can be paraphrased from [form]." You accept that an angelic apparition is an epiphany and a religious experience. The *presence* of Angel is the unveiling of a "blessed spirit," which will prove "rich with meaning and sanction ... blessing the land that had the wisdom to acknowledge him and make him welcome."[36]

Still, we should beware the fate of René Marqués' Abraham figure heeding Tony Kushner's warning in *Angels in America*: "An angel is just a belief, with wings and arms that can carry you. ... If it lets you down, reject it. Seek for something new." We must, "unblessed," face the angels with only love and courage to sustain us as we confront their numinous power.[37]

But where to find them? Where will they find us? We may expand Thomas Merton's comment about Emily Dickinson and consider "The poem ... *is* the Angel, the ladder of silver and gold by which hierophant and bard mount the world of the Imagination." Angel's manifestations ultimately must be forged in the labyrinth of the soul, where both angels and devils (who were once angels) reside as personal inhabitants. Angels will bring messages from beyond if we become aware of them (like Joseph), or wrestle nobly with them (like Jacob). Insistently, angelic contacts will lead to a delivery from the past and to the beholding of the future in the immediate present. "Magic," Borges reminds us, "is the crown or nightmare of the law of cause and effect. Not its contradiction."[38]

Notes

1 Federico García Lorca, "Teoría y juego del duende," in *Obras Completas* (Madrid: Aguilar, 1980), 1:1009. Translation by Giner.

2 Jorge Luis Borges, "A History of Angels," in *Selected Non-fictions*, ed. Eliot Weinberger (1926; New York: Penguin Books, 2000), 16–19. All Bible citations are from the Authorized King James Version (Cambridge).
3 García Lorca, "Teoría y juego del duende"; Sophocles, *Oedipus the King*, trans. Stephen Berg and Diskin Clay (New York: Oxford University Press, 1988), 85; Aristotle, *Poetics*, trans. Gerald Else (Ann Arbor: University of Michigan Press, 1973), 34–7.
4 Mary of Agreda, *City of God: The Divine History and Life of the Virgin Mother of God*, trans. Fiscar Marison (1670; Rockford, IL: Tan Books and Publishers, 1978), 225–6; Robert Louis Stevenson, *Dr. Jekyll and Mr. Hyde* (1886; New York: Bantam Books, 1985), 80; "The Annunciation," in *The Wakefield Mystery Plays*, ed. Martial Rose (New York: W. W. Norton, 1969), 178. For an overview of Medieval theater see A. M. Nagler, *The Medieval Religious Stage: Shapes and Phantoms* (New Haven: Yale University Press, 1976).
5 Federico Garcia Lorca, "San Gabriel (Sevilla)," *Obras Completas*, 1:415. Translation by Giner.
6 Carlos Blanco Aguinaga, Julio Rodríguez Puértolas, and Iris Zavala, *Historia social de la Literatura española* (Madrid: Editorial Castalia, 1979), 1:267; Santa Teresa de Jesús, *Su Vida* (1565; Madrid: Colección Austral, 1980), 165–6. Translation by Giner.
7 Quoted in Peter Lamborn Wilson, *Angels* (New York: Pantheon Books, 1980), 141; Christopher Marlowe, *Doctor Faustus: The 1604-Version Edition*, ed. Michael Keefer (Ontario: Broadview Press, 1995), 40; Stevenson, 79–81, 84.
8 Thomas Merton, *A Search for Solitude: The Journals of Thomas Merton, Volume Three 1952–1960*, ed. Lawrence S. Cunningham (New York: HarperSanFrancisco, 1996), 364; Emily Dickinson, *The Poems of Emily Dickinson*, ed. R. W. Franklin (1999; Cambridge: Harvard University Press, 2005), 218–19; Allen Tate, "New England Culture and Emily Dickinson," in *Bloom's BioCritiques: Emily Dickinson*, ed. Harold Bloom (Broomall, PA: Chelsea House Publishers, 2003), 119, 127. Italics in the original.
9 Jack Capps, quoted in Sandra McChesney, "A View from the Window: The Poetry of Emily Dickinson," and Kay Cornelius, "Biography of Emily Dickinson," in Bloom, 60, 37–8.
10 Doris Kearns Goodwin, *Team of Rivals: The Political Genius of Abraham Lincoln* (New York: Simon and Schuster, 2005), 335; Abraham Lincoln, "Letter to James H. Hackett, August 18, 1863," in *Speeches and Writings, 1859–1865*, ed. Don E. Fehrenbaher (New York: Library of America, 1989), 2:493; William Shakespeare, "Othello," in *The Yale Shakespeare: The Complete Works*, ed. Wilbur R. Cross and Tucker Brooke (New York: Barnes and Noble, 1993). Italics by Giner.
11 Goodwin, 326; Lincoln, "First Inaugural Address," in *Lincoln: Speeches and Writings*, 2:224. Italics by Giner.
12 F. B. Carpenter, *Six Months at the White House with Lincoln: The Story of a Picture* (1866; Watkins Glen, NY: Century House, 1961), 24–5.
13 Shakespeare, *Hamlet, Prince of Denmark*, ed. Philip Edwards (Cambridge: University Press, 2001).
14 Gore Vidal, *Lincoln: A Novel* (New York: Ballantine Books, 1984), 657.
15 Elizabeth Keckley, *Behind the Scenes. Or, Thirty Years a Slave, and Four Years in the White House* (1868; Oxford: University Press, 1988), 103; Carpenter, 46; Shakespeare, *The Life*

and *Death of King John* and *The Famous History of the Life of King Henry VIII*, ed. William H. Matchett and S. Schoenbaum (New York: Signet Classic Shakespeare, 2004).

16 Bernard Shaw, "Heartbreak House and Horseback Hall," preface to *Heartbreak House* (1919; Baltimore, MD: Penguin Books, 1974), 19; Drew Gilpin Faust, *This Republic of Suffering: Death and the American Civil War* (New York: Alfred A. Knopf, 2008), 139–40, 147; James Joyce, *A Portrait of the Artist as a Young Man* (1916; New York: Penguin Books, 1993), 268.

17 Soren Kierkegaard, *Fear and Trembling* (London: Penguin Books, 2003), 103, 137, 97, 139.

18 Euripides, *Iphigeneia at Aulis*, trans. W. S. Merwin and George E. Dimock, Jr. (New York: Oxford University Press, 1978), 79; Kierkegaard, 139, 114–15.

19 René Marqués, *Sacrificio en el Monte Moriah* (San Juan: Editorial Antillana, 1969), 47. Translations by Giner. For an overview of the works of Marqués, see Oscar Giner, "Exorcisms," *Theater*, 9, no. 3 (1978): 75–81; and Angelina Morfi, *Historia Crítica de un Siglo de Teatro Puertorriqueño* (San Juan: Instituto de Cultura Puertorriqueña, 1980), 455–514.

20 Ian Donaldson, *Ben Jonson: A Life* (New York: Oxford University Press, 2011), 188.

21 René Marqués, "El ruido y la furia de los críticos del Sr. Kazin" and "El puertorriqueño dócil," in *El puertorriqueño dócil y otros ensayos 1953–1971* (San Juan, PR: Editorial Antillana, 1977), 122–3 and 151–215. See https://borinqueneers.com/home (film).

22 Marqués, *Sacrificio*, 114–15 and "La leyenda hebrea de Abrahán, Sara e Isaac," in *Sacrificio*, 29; Kierkegaard, 139.

23 Kenneth Burke, *Attitudes Toward History* (1937; Berkeley: University of California Press, 1984), 225.

24 Marques, *Sacrificio*, 115–16.

25 Ibid., 134, 141.

26 Elaine Pagels, *The Origin of Satan* (New York: Random House, 1995), 39–40; Manuel Jover, *Caravaggio* (Paris: Editions TERRAIL/ÉDIGROUP, 2007), 90–3; Shakespeare, *King Lear* (Arden, 2003), 1.1.147.

27 Marqués, *Sacrificio*, 134.

28 Over the years, the university added the names of the Yale dead in other U.S. wars. Alison Frick, "The mingled dust of both armies," *Yale Alumni Magazine*, September/October 2011, https://yalealumnimagazine.com/articles/3279-the-mingled-dust-of-both-armies; Christopher Klein, "The Remarkable Story of Maya Lin's Vietnam Veterans Memorial," *Biography*, June 24, 2019, https://www.biography.com/news/maya-lin-vietnam-veterans-memorial.

29 Bao Ninh in Episode 1: "Déjà vu (1858–1961)," Ken Burns and Lynn Novick, *The Vietnam War* (PBS Series: Florentine Films, 2017); "The Virtual Wall," *Vietnam Veterans Memorial*, www.VirtualWall.org.

30 Ron Ferrizzi and John Musgrave, Episode 9: "A Disrespectful Loyalty (May 1970–March 1973)," in Burns and Novick, *The Vietnam War*.

31 Marc Chagall (1887–1985), *Abraham et les trois Anges*, Musée National Message Biblique Marc Chagall, Nice, France; Sor Juana Inés de la Cruz, *The Answer/La Respuesta, Including a Selection of Poems*, ed. and trans. Electa Arenal and Amanda Powell (New York: Feminist Press at the City University of New York, 1994), 54–5.

32 John Hersey, *Hiroshima* (1946; New York: Bantam Books, 1968), 7, 9, 15, 31.
33 John Huston, *The Bible: In the Beginning* (1966; 20th Century Fox, 2001).
34 "In Their Own Words: Who Said What When," *Frontline*, PBS, https://www.pbs.org/wgbh/pages/frontline/shows/truth/why/said.html.
35 A. A. Parker, *The Allegorical Drama of Calderón* (Oxford: Dolphin Book Co., 1968), 75–7; T. S. Eliot, "The Fire Sermon," in *Collected Poems 1909–1962* (1922; New York: Harcourt Brace Jovanovich, 1971), 60, 62. Shakespeare, *The Tempest* (New York: Signet, 1964).
36 William Arrowsmith, "Introduction," in Euripides, *Alcestis*, trans. William Arrowsmith (New York: Oxford University Press, 1989), 24–5; Richard Gilman, "Who Needs Critics" and "The Necessity of Destructive Criticism," in *Common and Uncommon Masks: Writings on Theatre—1961–1970* (New York: Vintage Books, 1972), 4, 18; Wilson, 101.
37 Tony Kushner, *Angels in America Part Two: Perestroika* (New York: Theatre Communications Group, 1996), 103; Arthur Miller, *After the Fall* (New York: The Viking Press, 1964), 113.
38 Wilson, 101; Borges, "History of Angels," 16–19, and "Narrative and the Art of Magic," 80 in *Selected Non-Fictions*.

· 5 ·

PASSAGE TO DEMOCRACY[1]

"After empire," to our way of thinking, is the arrested present, a landscape of dead but deadly metaphors, the prolonged period of U.S. imperialism. It is "a distillation and condensation of time and space," which is what occurs in a "developed mythic tradition."[2] "After" refers to the current reality, the immediate era of continuous warfare, when the attitude of militarism permeates political culture and plutocracy stifles democratic institutions and values. "Empire" is the present exigency to restore democracy. It is the crisis—the spiritual disturbance—that portends revelation, raised consciousness, conjuring of the better angels of the nation's democratic soul, and a symbolic reordering of polity and purpose.

Democratic Attitude

Democracy's renewal is a matter of attitude, both in the sense of what it means and the way it is practiced. What it signifies makes the difference between giving up on it in its enfeebled condition and unlocking its enduring spirit. Defining democracy as the rule of the people, primarily through their representatives and by majority vote in free and honest elections, is fair enough so far as it goes, yet lifeless without a corresponding sense of purpose. Absent purpose, democracy is an empty ritual, a process robbed of its chief value, a soulless institution, all of which dispirits and marginalizes the citizenry.

Walt Whitman understood that democracy is a richly symbolic word inflected with cultural value, a spiritual "password primeval," the rite of entry to our primal and intuitive soul, to our very identity as persons and as a people. "I am large, I contain multitudes," Whitman said of the democratic self. To him, democracy meant not accepting anything except what everyone else can have their "counterpart of on the same terms."[3] He could never get his fill of this kind of democracy, which resonated with overtones of equality among differences and resistance to privilege.

The democratic ideal is not elitist, discriminatory, or otherwise alienated from community, nor does it homogenize people. People are connected to one another on egalitarian terms and in continuing contestation of their interdependent differences. In this sense, democracy is a timeless myth of communion that transcends sheer individualism and opportunism. It is an emblem of political virtue and a dream of collective salvation, a true sentiment, a national quest, a recurring wish to restore power to the people for the good of the people.

The aspiration is dynamic. Democracy wholly institutionalized is democracy arrested and contained—form emptied of content, process dissociated from core values, and polity tamed. Democracy's fugitive vitality is stilled except in acts of dissent by which it might break out of imperial containment. Dissent prompts deliberation when it challenges how things presently stand, advocates change, and rallies supporters without vilifying outsiders and opponents, when it advances claims against the establishment consistent with democratic values. It constitutes democratic polity by speaking in an emotionally engaged, embodied voice of reason on behalf of fair dealing.[4]

As such, dissent is counterpoint to elite rule. It is the commons unbound—the living spirit of equality and community, fairness and justice, inclusion and interdependence of differences. It sustains democracy as a politics of contestation in which competing perspectives are held accountable to one another. It resists self-interested reasoning by the powers that be. It transcends alienation by engaging the community of several interests. The democratic self recognizes the humanity of its many faces. It does not make enemies readily or attribute evil to otherness effortlessly. It is inclined against demonizing others. Vilifying is not the democratic way of resisting militant imperialism.

Democracy by deliberative dissent—not to be confused with demagoguery—is a discourse that emanates from the margins, a diverse people's voice of accountability.[5] When understood as a curative practice for adding perspective, maintaining flexibility, and restoring balance, the problem of democracy is too little of it, not too much. We need more dissent, more deliberation, and more democracy to hold governing elites answerable to the people.

Empire's war culture constricts perspective and exaggerates differences to divide and alienate humanity. It transforms adversaries into enemies by obscuring their commonalities and ignoring their interdependencies. It forms a wall of militant orthodoxy built and sustained rhetorically to block the flow of humanity into democratic space.

Yet, walls of alienation built rhetorically can be breached rhetorically. Deliberative dissent maneuvers figuratively through the crevices of empire's rhetorical barriers to contravene demonizing stereotypes. It draws on metaphor to locate humanizing points of identification between fabricated foes. It deploys irony to fault empire's gratuitous caricatures, as in the paradox of a peace-loving country perpetrating global hostilities. Deliberative dissent follows the logic of similitude, reasoning by analogy to conclusions that are provisional instead of absolute. It puts the contingencies of circumstance and the complexity of perspective into play. Decisions reached by taking account of varied concerns and competing interests are necessarily conditional, non-totalizing, and thus subject to reconsideration.

Dissent that promotes deliberation and resists alienation in the pursuit of justice operates on the principle of a partial convergence of interests, identities, and agendas. It coordinates differences by articulating ways in which they are interdependent and complementary. Connections made among movements separately focused on issues such as gender equality, racial justice, environmental protection, economic wellbeing, and peacemaking are sufficiently selective, partial, and ambiguous to bring groups together provisionally without eliminating important distinctions. Such a diversity of complementary voices widens the field of resistance to the dehumanizing mindset of imperial belligerence. The passage to democracy runs through dissent from war conjoined with likeminded movements for social and environmental justice.

Hope and Lament

This is the conception of democracy by dissent, in the spirit of Old Man Coyote, that emerges from our mythopoetic journey over the turbulent landscape of imperial orthodoxy. We have heard the warrior's lament and channeled the better angels of political culture to grasp democracy anew neither fully realized nor hopelessly lost. By our reckoning, dissent operates on the premise of escape into democratic space through twists and turns of language, finding openings in empire's rhetorical barriers—barriers that alienate people from one another.

This view of democracy by dissent is positioned between the hope of building a strong foundation of democratic governance and the lament of democracy's imminent demise. It is neither adverse to a future of democratic governance, should that prove possible, nor indifferent to the degree of democracy's present decline. Indeed, dissent is a vehicle of escape from the menace of unmitigated authoritarianism and a means of passage to a more robust democratic demeanor and practice. It operates across a spectrum delineated by two poles. The positive pole is depicted in Josiah Ober's hypothetical "Demopolis," the negative in Eva Cherniavsky's dystopian image of neocitizenship. Together, they provide a paradigm of ambition in a context of menace, which clarifies dissent's immediate value for democratic renewal.

Despair over the undemocratic trajectory of political discourse drove *Washington Post* columnist E. J. Dionne, Jr. to utter a public prayer at the end of 2017, asking for democracy's "health and resurgence" in 2018.[6] His concern was reflected in Timothy Snyder's tract, also published in 2017, on tyranny's threat to the political order. Snyder insisted "the danger we now face is of a passage from … a naïve and flawed sort of democratic republic to a confused and cynical sort of fascist oligarchy."[7] At the beginning of 2018, Steven Levitsky and Daniel Ziblatt, examining the demise of liberal democracies in Europe, Latin America, and the U.S., argued that democracies succumb to totalitarianism from a prolonged weakening of the press, the judiciary, and other institutions, and from the deterioration of political norms including partisan and presidential restraint.[8] "Past stability," they warned, "is no guarantee of democracy's future survival."[9] Indeed, in January 2018, Jeff Flake, a despairing Republican Senator from Arizona, expressed his concern on the floor of the U.S. Senate over President Trump's use of "despotic language."[10] The day after Flake's speech, Freedom House released its annual report under the title "Democracy in Crisis." Michael Abramowitz's executive summary of the report observed that President Trump's "words and actions" contributed substantially to the erosion of democracy.[11] With the rise of Trumpism, the country fell deeper into the pit of a vulgar, hyperpolarizing political discourse.[12] By mid-2022, nearly half of the public polled did not believe the U.S.

would remain a democracy in the future, just as a group of historians met with President Biden to express their concern that democracy faced one of its most perilous threats in U.S. history.[13]

Short of succumbing to despair, Josiah Ober's thought experiment, entitled *Demopolis*, identified the conditions of basic democracy to resist the tyranny of polarization, racial strife, and exclusionary nationalism.[14] On the other hand, Eva Cherniavsky, working from the perspective of political culture, argued in her book on "neocitizenship" that "we are living in the midst of a momentous reconfiguration of political order." Democracy, from her standpoint, is a "deeply fraught formation," which "has been at once the object and the ground of left critique." Under the influence of neoliberalism, capitalist states, such as the U.S., have divorced democracy and "gravitated to oligarchical and autocratic forms of government." Democracy is dismantled. The "entrepreneurial citizen" must fend for herself under neoliberal rule as the state no longer claims to uphold the general interest of the people, and the public increasingly is dispersed into "nonintersecting planes of social existence and political imagining."[15]

Ober conceived the possibility, through civic education and deliberation, of establishing a solid foundation of democracy in support of liberal values. Cherniavsky perceived the present state of democracy as game over, perhaps. For her, neoliberalism's eclipse of popular sovereignty evokes a nightmarish image of the citizen reduced to a kind of simulacrum—a zombie or animated corpse, which advances relentlessly without faith or purpose. The state is no longer invested in producing public conviction or consent, or any kind of accountability to citizens and the common good. The question for Cherniavsky comes down to how to imagine political participation by neocitizens under neoliberal governance. Is any kind of resistance, protest, or dissent feasible when the state operates as a managerial apparatus sans accountability to a national body politic?[16] Can the de-democratized neocitizen, abandoned by the neoliberal state, act other than as a zombie figure of abjection?

Cherniavsky's answer seems to be that it is too soon to know whether citizenship somehow can be reconstituted and re-politicized under conditions of neoliberal rule. The people are dissociated rather than aggregated, reduced to singularities that are distributed along nonintersecting planes, and confronted with an unreadable world. The ground has shifted from under the citizenry, making it "difficult to discern the possibilities of opposition." Even the dissent of the earlier Occupy movement amounted to little more than establishing a communal ethos without a political aim. While something new is necessary,

Cherniavsky concluded, what might become "an alternative plane of political life ... outside the ruined institutions of modern democratic politics" is presently unknowable for lack of analytic resources to gauge what is emerging and because whatever it might become will take difficult political work to slowly emerge, if it emerges at all.[17]

Cherniavsky's poignant analysis of the demise of democratic citizenship points insightfully to a corresponding condition undercutting the deliberative function of political discourse. This condition—a condition of disarticulation—is illustrated in the George W. Bush administration's "case" for invading Iraq, a virulent instance of official reason being disconnected from a given and reproducible articulation of reality, thus making the rationale for regime change difficult to contest. It did not matter that no weapons of mass destruction could be found in Iraq because "the rationale was never embedded in a realist narrative framework." The "unreal" rationale for war amounted to "an array of disarticulated catchphrases and soundbites that functioned" like "staticky interference," an "unremitting flow of decontextualized narrative fragments, trigger points for a repertoire of intense but *dissociated* feeling" in a post-9/11 environment of patriotic sentiment and anti-Islamic feeling. This "political unreason" left people free "to assemble their views and sensibilities from a burgeoning menu of political memes and affects" (an eclectic array of themes such as Saddam threatened the U.S.; women must be saved from rape rooms; they hate our freedom; and so on). No attempt, no ideological gambit, was made by the administration to arrest the play of signifiers. While there was "no shortage of information," information no longer functioned ideologically to "*in-form*" the public or enable deliberation in the public interest.[18]

Cherniavsky's analysis of the reconfiguration of the contemporary political order and corresponding state of disarticulated political discourse poses a challenge for Ober's defense of democracy's deliberative potential. Ober contends that the promotion of liberty, equality, and dignity depends on realizing the human capacity for sociability, rationality, and communication. The heart of democratic practice is articulating the interdependence of individuals and groups with different and competing interests. Pluralism produces disagreement, which requires the exercise of strategic reason and communication to negotiate peacefully and productively—to construct motives for cooperation based on a perception of interdependence. Democracy requires a discourse of cooperation that promotes responsible deliberation of divisive issues, not a discourse of deception and manipulation that serves narrow self-interest. It requires a pro-social form of communication and persuasion to serve common-interest outcomes.[19]

Ober recognizes that the "stunted civic education" offered by the modern state "is unequal to the task of producing a capable demos," a deficiency that creates an opening for the rise of illiberal populism and despots. He invokes the image of Argos Panoptes, the many-eyed giant of Greek mythology, to warn a slumbering citizenry of the danger of tyranny. "Vigilance and readiness to respond" are the duties of a participating citizenry if they wish to preserve their democracy from the ever-present risk of elite capture. Argos "was bewitched into slumber and then killed in his sleep by ... Hermes at the behest of tyrannical Zeus." A vigilant citizenry, Ober cautioned, "must not be lulled into sleepy inattention."[20]

What happens when the delegated authority of elected representatives—delegation being a necessity of a large and complex modern state—is captured by elites to legislate in their own interests and against the common interests of the people? What happens when the sovereignty of the people is co-opted and democracy is corrupted? Ober warns the citizenry to exercise due diligence. The elected representatives of the people, he notes, are likely themselves to be elites prone "to promote elite interests against the common interests of the demos." Sans public scrutiny, the strong possibility exists "that a political class might coordinate to capture the government, becoming a de facto tyrant."[21]

Cherniavsky's insight reveals a state of political discourse that disarticulates, disaggregates, and disperses the citizenry, transforming them into depoliticized instrumentalities and singularities distributed along nonintersecting planes. The de-democratizing effect is due to a dearth of intersection among the citizenry. Ober's thought experiment attests to the centrality of the human capacity for communication as a vehicle for articulating the interdependence of diverse individuals and groups. Both are important perspectives on the problem and prospect of democracy. Each informs the other. Pushing too hard on the side of non-intersection risks declaring democracy's demise and oligarchy's triumph; counting too heavily on a discourse of cooperation risks succumbing to plutocracy's self-serving representation of reality and rational deliberation.

Ober's desire to conceptualize democracy as a stable system of governance sets aside Sheldon Wolin's fugitive democracy and Ernesto Laclau's and Chantal Mouffe's agonistic democracy.[22] Moreover, Cherniavsky, wishing to consider the "self-cultivation" of disaggregated agents rather than the forces and processes of constructing a people, chooses not to pursue Laclau's theory of populist reason, which Laclau conceives as a process of articulating disaggregated groups into a people by rhetorically constituting points of identification to enable singularities to work together politically.[23]

Something is gained, however, by taking account of both fugitive and agonistic models of democratic practice. They complement Ober's assessment of possibilities and address Cherniavsky's analysis of constraints. Wolin underscores democracy's episodic disposition; Laclau probes its rhetorical agency. Considered together, and in relationship to Ober and Cherniavsky, Wolin and Laclau suggest the deliberative potential of dissent. A tame and complacent democracy cannot meet the challenge of tyranny, whether the challenge emanates from neoliberal displacement of popular sovereignty and/or from illiberal populism. Dissent is an increasingly central feature of politics, observes Jeffrey Isaac, as a core value of liberal democracy that is key to resisting authoritarianism.[24] Democratic renewal requires deliberative dissent.

Deliberative Aptitude

Wolin's image of fugitive democracy emphasizes its occasional, ephemeral, circumstantial, local, and discordant character. It is politics concerned with the aspirations of the Many rather than the Few. As "a crystallized response to deeply felt grievances or needs," it "protests actualities and reveals possibilities." It opposes the anti-democratic structure and norms of the corporatist state.[25]

Wolin insisted that democracy's escape from containment by the corporatist state requires, in any given instance, transgressive acts.[26] Fugitive democracy is an undertaking of dissent aimed at reviving democracy, a political intervention on behalf of commonality against elite rule and elite rationality serving an elite economic polity.[27] In earlier fugitive moments of U.S. history, the demos acted against elite power to eliminate slavery, extend the right of voting to women, establish trade unions, oppose racial segregation, and resist war. Today, with society radically fragmented by economic interests, social classes, and cultural identities, there can be no unified demos, only various "democratic citizenries" to intervene on behalf of commonalities.[28]

Ober is correct, of course, in observing that Wolin did not concern himself with how democracy might govern in a traditional sense. Wolin explicitly doubted the possibility of sustaining collective self-rule in the late modern world. He believed democracy is born and reborn in transgressive acts—that the demos makes itself political and acquires a civic nature by transgressing boundaries, that democracy "seems destined to be a moment rather than a form," indeed, a "rebellious moment" that is "doomed to succeed only temporarily, but is a recurrent possibility" so long as "a belief in the restorative power of democracy is still part of the American political consciousness." Wolin's fugitive trades on democracy's recurring escape and renewal. While politics is ceaseless, the political is episodic, consisting of relatively rare moments of commonality "when, through public deliberations, collective power is used to promote or protect the well being of the collectivity."[29]

The figure of fugitive democracy is instructive in a climate of democratic decline and oligarchic rule because it combines dissent and deliberation rather than opposing one to the other, because it is a transgressive act to advance the claims and to consider the reasons of commonality, and because it is an act of democratic renewal. Even if we share Ober's vision of establishing a solid democratic foundation, we need to consider ways of recovering what has been lost.

While Wolin's fugitive democracy is transgressive for the purpose of advancing the rationale of commonality, Laclau's agonistic democracy is a project of articulating a people through nodal points of identification to allow for the intersection of singularities. He grounds popular reason in rhetorical contingency to advance an ensemble of claims against ruling elites. Popular reason consists of connecting heterogeneous claims through a metaphorical vision (or mythical fullness) sufficiently provisional to allow for deliberation by and among adversaries. Laclau understood that the construction of a people is integral to the prospect of democracy and that rhetoric is key to managing adversarial relations in pursuit of collective wellbeing.[30]

To articulate a collective identity in a heterogeneous political context is a hegemonic rhetorical act. The articulation of an ensemble of unmet demands brings a people into existence. The links in a chain of equivalences among otherwise diverse singularities are constructed rhetorically and thus are contingent. The links are named and invested by connecting metaphors, producing metaphorical totalizations, each with a trace of contingency—rather than a closed discourse, a complete representation, or an absolute truth. The tension between tenor and vehicle is never fully resolved in a metaphorical totalization that articulates a people framed by class, clan, nationality or some other more or less inclusive marker.

For Laclau, politics is a field crisscrossed by antagonistic forces. No one has complete and final answers, and there is no end of history. Struggles can solve particular problems partially, but no more than that. The clash of opinions, images, perceptions, ideas, values, and attitudes opens space for critical reflection, for deliberation, dialogue, negotiation, partial conversion, and ongoing struggle. The articulation of a people is never a fully universal or a final representation of the people. It is tropologically achieved—a product of catachresis, a violation of convention—to promote a lively contestation of beliefs and perspectives in which adversaries are not reduced to sheer enemies. Laclau's notion of populist reason encompasses collective deliberation and liberal values of human rights and individual liberty along with democratic values of equality, community, and popular sovereignty. As a function of contingency, populist democratic reason resists head-on, non-negotiable confrontation with adversaries, while populist rhetorical hegemony serves as a corrective to a repressive political order. It is dissent that subverts and reconstructs within the constraints of the central ordering practices of a society and political culture.

The rhetorical character of Laclau's conception of popular reason, specifically the operation of metaphors that provisionally link singularities to one another, speaks to the problem Cherniavsky identifies as neoliberalism's disaggregation and dispersal of the citizenry into non-intersecting planes of social existence and political imagining. Laclau treats the condition of non-intersection as a rhetorical challenge and shifts the issue from a problem of ruling elites undermining deliberation by failing to arrest the play of signifiers, as in the case of the Bush administration's war rhetoric, to a project of dissenting by popular reason produced tropologically, that is, democratic reason born in similitude. In Laclau's view, deliberation, "conceived in a wide sense (involving partial conversions, dialogues, negotiations, struggles, and so on)," is inherent to the collective process of rhetorical construction. "For what a truth which is less than total will be confronted with is other opinions, views, ideas, and so on—and if the truth is *permanently* non-total it will have to incorporate into its form this element of confrontation, which involves collective deliberation."[31] The deliberative potential of contingent rhetorical hegemony supplants the unreason of neoliberalism's imperial divorce from democracy.

Democratic Openings

If we follow leads from Wolin and Laclau, the possibility of democratic renewal would seem to reside in a nonconformist and paradoxical political discourse. These two traits, along with their entailments of contingency, connectivity, discordance, and escape from elite containment, suggest a rhetorical hybrid of dissent enabling deliberation. Deliberative dissent is a democratic act of articulating commonality and collectivity amid diversity and pluralism, of constructing a non-totalizing political bond in a heterogeneous context, and of advancing a hegemonic struggle over demands against a state under elite control, a state that is unresponsive to the concerns, requests, and claims of the citizenry.

Conceived in this way, deliberative dissent, operating on a discursive plane dominated by the few, escapes containment partially and momentarily by maneuvering around, over, under, and through barriers that separate and disperse citizens.[32] It seeks openings into democratic spaces of interdependence. The contingent or provisional quality of an articulation of the people is catachrestic in its deliberate "misuse" of terms, creating a paradox by means of a trope—by a twist or turn on conventional language to alter meaning. The turn of the trope is at once strange and recognizable as it subverts the barrier of undemocratic norms and opens space to form linkages among disaggregated identities. Catachresis exploits the pores of political discourse, the in-between spaces, to allow singularities to connect in non-totalizing relations of interdependence. It enables the coordination of differences.

Deliberative dissent is a hybrid discourse that is itself a trope, an oxymoron, a condensed paradox. It operates tropologically in discursive space to mediate division and alienation by articulating provisional, non-totalizing chains of equivalence, which allows for a degree of tolerance and cooperation in advancing claims for social justice. A sense of a people emerges in mutually conditioning linkages among identities. Kriti Sharma refers to this kind of interdependence as a relationship of "contingentism" in which entities do not just interact but rather are mutually constituted. The conditional existence of each entity in a network of relations depends on the conditional existence of other entities.[33] Parts constitute and exist within a whole; elements supplement or balance one another.

Tropes open spaces in which contingent linkages of interdependence can form by revealing connections that conventional discourse obscures. Tropes enable us to see possible relations that habitude blocks from view. They articulate the "Aha!" moment of seeing something anew.

Metaphor combines two terms creatively—unconventionally—to suggest a shared quality or similarity among distinct, ostensibly unlike entities, creating a fresh combination of ideas in which a literalized term (a tenor) is refigured by another term (a vehicle), each term animating the other. In the dead metaphors of U.S. war culture, enemies are routinely dehumanized and habitually demonized. Grasping the humanity of enemies involves refiguring them, for instance, within the familial web of brothers and sisters. Such a move is not culturally incoherent, but it is unconventional in the context of empire.

Metonymy and synecdoche are similar in form and function. While synecdoche is sometimes considered a type of metonymy, Kenneth Burke distinguishes between the general case of synecdochic convertibility and the special case of metonymic reductionism. Either way, these tropes are concerned principally with relations of contiguity, including part to whole, container and contained, sign and signified, cause and effect, and genus and species.[34] A sympathetic sense of connectivity between nuclear antagonists, for instance, might be glimpsed in the instant of representing North Korea as the container of its people (synecdoche) rather than reducing it metonymically to its dictator.

The trope of irony points to inconsistency. Two terms that are normally presumed to go together or to be alike are revealed as contradictory or contrary in some way. When speaking of a good Us vs. a bad Them, a sense of irony can come from noting the supposedly heartless enemy's anguish and/or the heartlessness of one's own presumably beneficent country. Irony bedevils overgeneralizations, stereotypes, and abstractions with contradictory details, exceptions, deviations, and disjunctions. Donald Trump's border wall, built on the dehumanizing stereotype of criminality, does not account well for undocumented immigrants and asylum seekers working hard, paying taxes, and obeying laws in the U.S. after escaping from violence in their home countries and braving the hazards of migration to protect and reunite their families. These are not the behaviors of sinister criminals.

These four figures—metaphor, metonymy, synecdoche, and irony—are the master tropes, but other figures, such as personification, hyperbole, euphemism, and oxymoron, also can create provisional openings and connections to promote deliberative dissent. Tropological insights are starting points for articulating lines of argument by analogy, definition, or cause and effect.

In the context of resisting war culture, a tropological impetus for an argument of interdependence is especially relevant to democratic renewal. To deliberate a restructuring of the war state requires the articulation of a citizenry that grasps the relationship of imperial warfare to an array of socio-economic inequities. Positive peace, contrary to war culture, consists of a mosaic of attitudes, beliefs, values, and institutional patterns that promote nonviolent management of conflict based on equitable wealth sharing, environmental sustainability, an appreciation of diversity, and a robust sense of interdependence.[35] Images of interdependence are central to expressing concerns over environmental degradation, economic displacement, systemic discrimination, and other issues of structural violence in opposition to an attitude of exceptionalism and a corresponding discourse of wealth and security obtained by global domination. A case in point is the murder of George Floyd by a Minneapolis police officer on May 25, 2020, which was caught on video by a teenaged girl.[36] It set in motion a nationwide protest against the systemic racism and brutality of militarized police forces, both of which are endemic to war culture and empire.

To open to democratic critique a militaristic discourse of white privilege and economic elitism requires a language that envisions a commons in metaphorical terms of partnership, teamwork, family, friendship, neighborhood, community, and other networks. Martin Luther King, Jr. opposed poverty, racism, and militarism by envisioning "a beautiful symphony of brotherhood" and a "worldwide fellowship that lifts neighborly concern."[37] Howard Zinn drew on a metaphor of kinship to link the problem of war with an array of social issues, conveying a vision of "one human family" that joined the concerns of women, workers, minorities, the poor, and immigrants. He argued that humans historically have pursued in creative ways "a yearning for community" that rejects violence.[38] Veterans for Peace spoke suggestively of an "epidemic" of violence, an image that links U.S. wars abroad to a domestic record of slavery, war on indigenous peoples, racist immigration policies, economic violence against the poor of all colors, and militarization of the police. In this connecting metaphor of infectious violence, confronting militarism entails confronting racism, sexism, poverty, climate change, and other issues of socio-economic degradation and oppression.[39]

Tropological openings are windows of opportunity for developing an awareness of intersection into an attitude of interdependence, for constructing a democratic commons with a contingent logic of similitude, contiguity, and contradiction, for crafting a degree of identification and coordination to compensate for the prevailing condition of division and dispersal that undermines democratic praxis. The tropo-logic of deliberative dissent enables democratic discourse by making openings that never fully close. Catachrestic openings resist the totalizing discourse of economic elites who rule by separating and scattering the demos. Responding to the disaggregation of the citizenry with figures of connectivity to confound alienating barriers of separation is an unruly act of dissent with deliberative potential.

Enacting Positive Peace by Deliberative Dissent

Dissent discharges a democratic impulse in the here and now of imperial war culture. With a humanizing gesture to circumvent the caricature of adversaries as monsters, deliberative dissent reframes its demands in affirmative terms to avoid entrapment in a negative cycle of vilification. Humanizing gestures access democratic values of inclusion, fairness, and wellbeing, the values of community that blur the polarities of animus and animate the pursuit of social justice. The logic of similitude prompts empathy by highlighting similarities among differences. It identifies through likeness, instead of sameness, to loosen the manacles of fear and hatred that restrain political affinity.

Escape from the alienation of imperial war culture into democratic space is the immediate undertaking of deliberative dissent. Escape leads toward peace. Step by step, deliberative dissent enacts positive peace. It epitomizes peacemaking in a dynamic context of conflicted interests and an ongoing process of advancing claims for social justice.

Deliberative dissent corresponds to positive peace on several counts. A culture of peace, beyond the mere absence of military violence, promotes human fulfillment and collective wellbeing. It strives for an absence of the structural violence of human exploitation. Unlike empire's coerced peace, it strives to manage conflict nonviolently, pursuing peace by peaceful means. It consists of a web of constitutive discourses (a mosaic of assumptions, axioms, attitudes, beliefs, values, identities, and institutional patterns) to address issues of injustice and reduce threatening perceptions of extreme otherness.[40] The deliberative attributes of dissent grounded in rhetorical contingency and committed to democratic values are vital to the pursuit of positive peace.

Democratic dissent and peace building are both dynamic and deliberative; they manage tensions among differences in an ongoing process informed by principles of equity and nonviolence and leading to contingent rather than totalizing outcomes. Enacting positive peace involves making deliberative dissent's double gesture of limited nonconformity, of disagreement balanced by concurrence, disruption by affirmation, dissonance by reassurance. Transgressing the prevailing mindset is offset by embracing something recognizable, understandable, and socially sanctioned, something that connects contesting sides in democratic space to forestall vilification, alienation, and violence.[41] Tropes make the contingent linkages that accommodate political pluralism. They are the mythic spirits of creative boundary crossing, the linguistic turns out of divisive formations, the vehicles that reconfigure and legitimate estranged parties.

As with dissent's fugitive pursuit of democracy, the development of peace culture is episodic and cumulative but incomplete and impermanent in the foreseeable future. The spirit that persists in the millennial dream of positive peace sustains continuing resistance to the violence and injustice of imperial war culture. In the meantime, resistance by deliberative dissent contributes a democratic voice of fairness and inclusion and provides a channel of escape from the alienation that sustains the rule of imperial violence.

How does this ongoing exercise in democratic dissent look for pursuing positive peace in the immediate context of imperial war culture? No single example can represent fully the myriad openings into democratic space, but the process can be clarified by way of a suggestive example. Accordingly, we end our account of these exigent times with an illustration of enacting positive peace by deliberative dissent. Our illustration, understandably, is as rhetorical as it is factual so that it might be rendered more meaningful, heuristic, and truthful. Such is the way of a mythopoetic intervention inspired by Old Man Coyote, who remakes the world via boundary crossings, and Abraham's angels, which exist within the democratic soul to be conjured up in circumstances of crisis.

Prosopopoeia

> And if we do act, in however small a way, we don't have to wait for some grand utopian future. The future is an endless succession of presents, and to live now as we think humans should live, in defiance of all that is bad around us, is itself a marvelous victory.
>
> Howard Zinn[42]

Prosopopoeia is the rhetorical figure of giving voice to an imaginary, absent, or dead person in language consistent with the character of the person and appropriate to the subject and circumstances—representing such a person as if she or he is real, present, alive, and capable of speaking and hearing. Its relationship to the figure of personification is especially relevant to resisting imperial war culture democratically. War rhetoric, which alienates one party from another in dehumanizing, demonizing, and de-civilizing terms, requires the re-personifying corrective afforded by prosopopoeia. The future of peacemaking exists in an endless succession of personifications that defy the alienating discourse of war.

In the spirit of prosopopoeia, Howard Zinn recovered myriad voices of the people. He was a World War II veteran, revisionist historian, political playwright, and social activist who operated at the intersection of democracy, dissent, and war. He exposed the absence of voices, voices unrepresented in standard accounts of war's necessity, heroics, and triumph. In Zinn's account, the paradox of war—its ironic contradictions—troubled its rationalization, even in the case of World War II—the national archetype of the good war, the just war, the war for democracy and liberty. Irony destabilized the contrastive features of the dehumanizing war narrative. Prosopopoeia restored the humanity of the displaced commons.

Zinn slipped out of the trap of the good-war storyline by locating contradictions between what was said and what went unsaid. He was initially ensnared by the call to arms in defense of democracy. As a bombardier in World War II, he flew B-17 missions over France, Germany, Hungary, and Czechoslovakia. He didn't like war, but he joined in the fight against Fascism because he believed this war was "a people's war, a war against the unspeakable brutality of Fascism." Unlike other wars, this war "was not for profit or empire":

> What could be more justifiable than a war against Fascism, which was ruthlessly crushing dissent at home, and taking over other countries, while proclaiming theories of racial supremacy and promoting a spirit of nationalist arrogance. When Japan, which was committing atrocities in China, allied itself to Italy and Germany, and then attacked the U.S. fleet at Pearl Harbor, it seemed to be clear—it was the democratic countries against the Fascist countries.[43]

Eventually, based on his experience and historical research, Zinn changed his mind about World War II and war in general.

World War II was the supreme test of whether there is such a thing as a just war.[44] How could the U.S. claim to fight a war to protect the rights of nations to independence and self-determination when it had a long history of expansion through war and conquest, and when it waited so long to intervene against Fascist expansion? Isn't this a sign of hypocrisy? Or was it really a just war to defend self-determination, oppose racism, save the Jews, and secure democracy?

Zinn identified multiple destabilizing inconsistencies in the story of the good war. On the matter of self-determination, President Roosevelt's and Prime Minister Churchill's Atlantic Charter promised a postwar world of national independence to court the support of the nonwhite colonial world— a world colonized by the likes of Britain, France, Holland, and Belgium—even as the U.S. Secretary of State gave the French private assurances that they could reclaim their colony of Indochina after the war. The aim of the war was not to change Europe or the world but to get rid of Hitler and his allies. And it was an opportunity to give U.S. business a leg up in Middle East oil and other enterprises when the British were too weakened by the war to maintain their old empire. The war launched the "American century."[45]

What about fighting against the Nazi notion of a superior race? U.S. armed forces, like the country in general, were segregated by race; black soldiers and sailors were largely relegated to menial tasks and otherwise discriminated against in the military. Japanese residing in the U.S., most of whom were U.S. citizens, were rounded up and confined to concentration camps, euphemistically referred to as relocation camps. They lost their freedom and their property.[46] Roosevelt shunted the issue of Hitler's assault on Jews to the U.S. State Department, which assigned the problem a low priority and continued to stall even when, as late as August 1942, Jewish leader Stephen Wise brought its attention to evidence of the ongoing holocaust.[47]

What about fighting for freedom and democracy? Dissenters in the U.S. were sent to prison, workers' wages were frozen, and soaring corporate profits concentrated wealth in fewer hands. Social reform was not on the agenda.[48]

What about atrocities? Is a war just when both sides commit atrocities? The Nazis murdered millions of Jews. The U.S. and its allies indiscriminately bombed cities, as did Germany and its allies. Massive airstrikes against German civilians aimed to lower their morale. The saturation bombing of Dresden alone created a firestorm that suffocated 100,000 people. Another 100,000 people died when the city of Tokyo was reduced to ashes. And then came the atomic bombing of Hiroshima and Nagasaki. The moral line was crossed. "It seems that once an initial judgment has been made that a war is just, there is a tendency to stop thinking, to assume then that everything done on behalf of victory is morally acceptable," Zinn ruefully observed.[49]

What did the victory over Fascism bring about? Two superpowers emerged to vie with one another for world domination, "carving out new spheres of influence, on a scale even larger than that attempted by Fascist powers. Both superpowers supported dictatorship all over the world."[50] And wars continued to flare up in Korea, Vietnam, Nicaragua, Nigeria, Iraq, and elsewhere. Thus, the Good War in Zinn's ironic perspective is a cautionary tale:

> The practical effect of declaring World War II *just* is not for that war but for the wars that follow. And that effect has been a dangerous one, because the glow of rightness that accompanied that war has been transferred, by false analogy and emotional carryover, to other wars. To put it another way, perhaps the worst consequence of World War II is that it kept alive the idea that war could be just.[51]

War, even the so-called good war, corrupts everyone and everything it touches. It poisons the minds and souls of combatants on all sides. It is a process that makes us "unthinking killers of innocent people. A decision is made at the start of a war that your side is good and the other side is bad, and once you make that decision you don't have to think any more; anything you do, no matter how horrible, is acceptable."[52]

Several fallacies are embedded in the logic of war. One is that our side is good because the other side is evil. Another is that a just cause legitimizes the ravages of war, which maims and kills the very people we would liberate from a tyrant. By far, most of the victims of modern wars have been civilians. War is indiscriminate destruction and killing. It cannot be humanized, no matter how it is justified or celebrated. It does not change the world for the better. And its prospect is increasingly horrendous with "advances" in killing technologies. The internal contradiction, the irony, of a war on terrorism is that "war itself is terrorism."[53]

Zinn found and represented voices in the interstices exposed by the paradox of war, recognizable voices that crossed over boundaries of nationality, color, ethnicity, gender, and class and into the democratic commons. Zinn's voices of the people complicated the dehumanizing pretexts of warfare. They personified the victims of violence. They made common cause against injustice one instance after another in resolute succession.

In 1966, Zinn returned to Royan, the French seaside resort he had helped to obliterate 21 years earlier. His flight of bombers dropped napalm over the area. It was saturation bombing, not specifically aimed at the German troops garrisoned in and near the town. It seemed at the time "just another bombing mission." Zinn was "completely unaware of the human chaos below." The devastating attack occurred three weeks before the final surrender of Germany, "at a time when everyone knew" the war in Europe soon would end. Royan was located far from the fighting. It commanded a sea entrance on the Atlantic unimportant to the war effort. Napalm was a new weapon, previously untested in warfare. As Zinn the historian concluded, "The evidence seems overwhelming that factors of pride, military ambition, glory, honor were powerful motives in producing an unnecessary military operation." The military machine needlessly sacrificed "human flesh and sense" in the service of "abstractions of duty and obedience."[54] No one in the system threw a wrench in the machinery to disrupt the false crusade.

Zinn found most of the material for his own dissent on behalf of the victims in rebuilt Royan's town library. He recovered there a little book of documents—one of the documents describing the horror of the bombing—produced and printed in Royan by a former member of the French Resistance. "For Royannais," a local wrote, "this liberation by force was useless" since Royan soon would have been liberated "without new damage, without new deaths, without new ruins." One must visit Royan to know the disaster. "No report, no picture or drawing can convey it." This attack, wrote another local, was "a deadly work of obvious uselessness." A former Resistance leader and Mayor of Royan, rejecting a French General's explanation that the attack was necessary to prevent the Germans from surrendering on their own as if they were unconquered, retorted:

> The Germans had to feel our power! Permit me, my general, to tell you, once and for all, in the name of those who paid the cost: "La Victoire de Royan' does not exist, except for you."[55]

As a vehicle of dissent, prosopopoeia afforded Zinn a way of complicating war's undemocratic obfuscations.

In the same way, when the U.S. attacked Iraq in 1998, Zinn "cut through the abstraction of bombing" by way of an email he received from an Iraqi citizen, Dr. Mohammed Al-Obaidi, who was taking refuge in the U.K. from Saddam Hussein's brutal regime. Al-Obaidi had lost his father and youngest brother to Saddam's brutality:

> I am writing to you to let you know … a cruise missile hit my parents' house in the suburb of Baghdad. My mother, my sister-in-law (wife of my deceased brother), and her three children were all killed instantly.
>
> Such a tragedy shocked me to such an extent I lost my tears. I am crying without tears. I wish I could show my eyes and express my severe and painful suffering to every American and British [citizen]. I wish I could tell my story to those sitting in the American Administration, the U.N., and at Number 10 Downing Street.

Humanizing war's victims, re-personifying them by conveying Al-Obaidi's tragic story, put Americans in correspondence with the Iraqi doctor, linking them across national boundaries in solidarity and resistance to governments on both sides that "visit death and suffering on the people."[56] America's claim to democracy was "being shattered by the rush to war," Zinn maintained, "by allowing a small number of political leaders to push the American people into war without a real national debate, without a full airing of the issues." Indeed, "if the American people had access to the facts, could listen to the different points of view, and [had] time for reasoned judgment, they would call a halt to our leaders' lust for violence."[57]

By way of these and many other examples, Zinn hailed the voice of the people to make war accountable to its victims. There is no just war, Zinn maintained in a talk he gave in Rome on June 23, 2005. The problem is the persistence of war, a challenge that must be taken up by the people of the world, which is a democratic challenge. Citizens of war-making nations must play their part as members of the human family pursuing a vision of a different world in which they do not sacrifice their children to the war machine. There is no instinct for war.[58] On the contrary:

> It is a tribute to the natural instincts of people, to preserve life, to care for other people, that governments must use all the powers at their command—bribery, coercion, propaganda—to overcome those natural instincts and persuade a nation that it must go to war.[59]

Propaganda is empire's most powerful weapon in mobilizing populations for war. The grand abstractions of war rhetoric "say nothing about human beings." They call for obedience in the name of democracy while acting against the principles of democracy. Obedience to the state is the essence of totalitarianism. Disobedience by dissent is required when a so-called democracy acts against life, liberty, and the pursuit of happiness.[60] War propaganda constructs unnatural barriers between members of the human family.

Zinn wrote history "to awaken a great consciousness of racial injustice, sexual bias, class inequality, and national hubris," to "bring into the light the unreported resistance of people against the power of the Establishment," and "to illustrate the creative power of people struggling for a better world." He told the stories of people who stood up, spoke out, and connected to one another. He emphasized new possibilities by "disclosing those hidden episodes from the past when, even in brief flashes, people showed their ability to resist, to join together, and occasionally to win." A better future, he supposed, might be found in these past "fugitive moments of compassion" rather than in more warfare. "Change in public consciousness," he wrote, comes about when people begin to connect multiple dots of discontent.[61]

Zinn's revisionist history featured the voices of the people, dissenting voices on a wide spectrum of social issues, voices not present in the mainstream history that is written from the perspective of power elites.[62] He represented the diverse people of the commons, often in their own words, in their distinct grievances and their intersecting interests, the people past and present who "keep alive the spirit of resistance to injustice and war"—the mostly unremembered and unnoticed heroes "who have, often in the most modest ways, spoken out and acted on their beliefs for a more egalitarian, more just, peace-loving society."[63]

Zinn's figure of prosopopoeia recovers what is absent, gives presence to what is missing, across the spectrum of injustice because "the invisibility of the 'other' carries over into war, where the 'enemy' is other than human."[64] To read Zinn's history, written from a people's perspective, is to hear the many voices missing from standard histories, each a separate cause until it meets at the crossroads of democratic dissent.

The problem that prompts dissent is a narrow nationalism, which sustains imperial war culture by proclaiming a moral purpose of defending and promoting democracy, protecting liberty and saving lives, eliminating weapons of mass destruction, stopping the spread of totalitarianism, and/or defeating terrorism. All of this diverts attention from domestic issues while spreading U.S. power around the globe to control vital resources "in the interests of corporate profit." The twenty-first century American imperium, Zinn observed, is "a global hegemony whose grace notes are free markets, human rights, and democracy." The symbols of aggressive nationalism reflect and sustain the myth that, in Zinn's words, "our nation is different from, morally superior to, the other imperial powers of world history."[65] Lacking historical perspective, the U.S. citizenry is penned inside the boundaries of nationalism by the "arrogant perspective" that the U.S. "is the center of the universe, exceptionally virtuous, admirable, superior." Americans are assured that their moral superiority is good reason to dominate the world.[66]

The injustices perpetrated by imperial war culture may seem overwhelming and beyond the reach of democratic change for the better, but persistent dissent is warranted, Zinn argued, not because one can be totally confident the state of the world will improve. Continuing to dissent is motivated instead by a determination "not to give up the game until all the cards have been played." Life is a gamble one must take to create the possibility of change, change that comes about "through an endless succession of surprises, moving zigzag toward a more decent society."[67] That is Zinn's "optimism of uncertainty" in resisting the dehumanizing discourse of war by speaking in myriad voices missing from the narrative of American exceptionalism.

Peroration

Imperial war culture is undemocratic. It privileges the interests of the few over the many and alienates the many from one another. The people and their claims against governing elites are dispersed, held away from democratic space by the vilifying discourse of the war state. The internal other is projected onto the external enemy. Likewise, dissent abandons democracy when it dehumanizes and demonizes in the service of totalizing truths that prevent people from deliberating with one another. Dissent in the spirit of democracy is inclusive. It opens space for the convergence of human interests, intersections of interdependence that provide common ground and engender respect for differences.

The passage to democracy leads away from the culture of war. Zinn's figure of prosopopoeia, though not definitive, is illustrative and suggestive. It personifies in the spirit of solidarity by recovering lost voices and reconnecting the human family across divisions of race, gender, class, religion, and nationality. It emerges in the paradox of war and resonates with the metaphor of kinship. As it expands the democratic self and amplifies the voice of the people, it reduces the degree of alienation constructed by the war narrative of power elites. It elucidates by example the way in which irony, metaphor, and other tropes and figures can escape the confines of war culture's rhetorical barrier, creating openings into democratic space, a space of egalitarian interdependence in which a people come together to make common cause for peace and justice.

There is no straight line of progress from imperial war culture to a democratic culture of positive peace. Democracy by dissent is the fugitive proclivity of Old Man Coyote. It is ongoing. Its dynamic is rhetorical contingency, which makes it open to competing perspectives. The guiding image of democracy and peace is partially realized by acts of deliberative dissent in the here and now of imperial war culture. Each enactment in kind is a momentary escape from alienation, another example for others to follow. The passage to democracy is an immediate, momentary, and case-by-recurring-case of enacting positive peace in deliberative dissent.

Democratic convergence is a process, not a stable state. It is an open-ended process of deliberative dissent under conditions of elite rule. The democratic spirit of inclusion lives by dissent. It holds privilege accountable within governing institutions as well as on the streets and places in between. Form follows function. Dissent functions as the voice of a people, in several intersecting registers. Its form balances contingent gestures, one a demand for justice and the other a word of solidarity. Its mythic fullness is expressed in humanizing metaphors of kinship, friendship, partnership, community, and other networks of interdependence. The twists and turns of its tropes and figures provide catachrestic escape into democratic space. It happens now. Each deliberative moment of democratic dissent is a conjuring of better angels, a reconsideration, a redirection, a different understanding, a beginning, the dawning of a new symbolic order, all of which requires a stripping away of old habits of mind following an internal struggle and divestiture of the ornaments of empire. Each step in a tenuous passage to democracy is taken in the spirit of a just and inclusive peace.

Notes

1. This chapter draws in part from and reworks Robert L. Ivie and Oscar Giner, "A Democratic People's Dissent from War," *Javnost—The Public* 24, no. 3 (2017): 199–217, and Robert L. Ivie, "Democratic Spaces of Interdependence," *China Media Research* 12 (2017): 17–27.
2. Robert Bringhurst, *The Tree of Meaning: Language, Mind and Ecology* (Berkeley: Counterpoint, 2008), 55.
3. Walt Whitman, "Song of Myself," Sections 24, 51, in *Leaves of Grass* (1891–92; New York: Barnes and Noble, 2004), 214, 250.

4 For a discussion of the tension between the norms of civility and dissent for social justice, see Andrew Calabrese, "Liberalism's Disease: Civility above Justice," *European Journal of Communication* 30, no. 5 (2015): 539–53.
5 Right-wing authoritarian demagoguery by the likes of Donald Trump is often conflated with populism and democracy. Democratic populism, on the other hand, signifies self-government and the common interest of the many over the special interests of the rich and powerful. See, for example, Christian Fuchs, "Authoritarian Capitalism, Authoritarian Movements and Authoritarian Communication," *Media, Culture & Society* 40, no. 5 (2018): 780.
6 E. J. Dionne, Jr., "The Real Greatest Threat to Democracy This Year," *Washington Post*, December 28, 2017, https://www.washingtonpost.com/opinions/the-real-greatest-threat-to-democracy-this-year/2017/12/27/a74375e8-eb28-11e7-9f92-10a2203f6c8d_story.html?utm_term=.9ea474600a26.
7 Timothy Snyder, *On Tyranny: Twenty Lessons from the Twentieth Century* (New York: Tim Duggan Books, 2017), 124.
8 Steven Levitsky and Daniel Ziblatt, *How Democracies Die* (New York: Penguin Random House, 2018).
9 Steven Levitsky and Daniel Ziblatt, "Is Donald Trump a Threat to Democracy?" *New York Times*, December 16, 2016, https://www.nytimes.com/2016/12/16/opinion/sunday/is-donald-trump-a-threat-to-democracy.html?emc=edit_ty_20180104&nl=opinion-today&nlid=1307871&te=1&_r=0.
10 CBS News, "Transcript: Sen. Jeff Flake's [sic] Speaks about the Dangers of Calling Facts 'Fake News,'" January 17, 2018, https://www.cbsnews.com/news/jeff-flake-speech-trump-rebuke-senate-full-transcript/.
11 Michael J. Abramowitz, "Democracy in Crisis," *Freedom House*, January 18, 2017, https://freedomhouse.org/report/freedom-world/freedom-world-2018#anchor-one. Also see Simon Tisdall, "American Democracy is in Crisis, and Not Just Because of Trump," *The Guardian*, August 8, 2018, https://www.theguardian.com/commentisfree/2018/aug/07/american-democracy-crisis-trump-supreme-court?utm_source=esp&utm_medium=Email&utm_campaign=GU+Today+USA+-+Collections+2017&utm_term=283011&subid=1405707&CMP=GT_US_collection.
12 For a sustained critique of Trumpism, see Jeffrey C. Isaac, *#AgainstTrump: Notes From Year One* (New York: Public Seminar Books, 2018). For an analysis of the undemocratic, racist tropes that define Trumpist rhetoric, see Robert L. Ivie, "Dissenting Democratically from Trump's Toxic Tropes," *Javnost–The Public*, 30, no. 1 (2023): 1–13. For an overview of Trump's rhetoric and its implications for democracy, see Robert C. Rowland, *The Rhetoric of Donald Trump: Nationalist Populism and American Democracy* (Lawrence: University of Kansas Press, 2021).
13 Ivie, "Dissenting Democratically," 1–2. For an indication of how conservative and right-ward leaning Republicans see the threat to democracy, see Gary Abernathy, "Fear for Our Democracy Runs Both Ways, But Only Half of That Story Gets Told," *Washington Post*, April 18, 2023, https://www-washingtonpost-com.proxyiub.uits.iu.edu/opinions/2023/04/18/democracy-trump-republicans-democrats-socialist/.

14 Josiah Ober, *Demopolis: Democracy before Liberalism in Theory and Practice* (Cambridge, UK: Cambridge University Press, 2017), 177–80.
15 Eva Cherniavsky, *Neocitizenship: Political Culture after Democracy* (New York: New York University Press, 2017), 1–4, 10. Deepa Kumar argues that raced, gendered, and classed neoliberal national security discourse prepares the public to assume the role of imperial citizens: "National Security Culture: Gender, Race, and Class in the Production of Imperial Citizenship," *International Journal of Communication* 11 (2017): 2154–77.
16 Cherniavsky, 16, 32, 68, 138–9.
17 Cherniavsky, 152, 154–5, 160, 162, 188, 192, 194.
18 Cherniavsky, 141–4. Emphasis in the original.
19 Ober, 87–8, 104–8.
20 Ober, 130, 161, 180.
21 Ober, 132, 155.
22 Ober, 15, 167.
23 Cherniavsky, 191–2.
24 Isaac, *#Against Trump*, 143, 172, 304.
25 Sheldon S. Wolin, *Politics and Vision*, expanded edition (Princeton, NJ: Princeton University Press, 2004), 601–6.
26 Sheldon S. Wolin, "Fugitive Democracy," in *Democracy and Difference: Contesting the Boundaries of the Political*, ed. Seyla Benhabib (Princeton, NJ: Princeton University Press, 1996), 33, 37, 43.
27 Sheldon S. Wolin, *Democracy Incorporated: Managed Democracy and the Specter of Inverted Totalitarianism* (Princeton, NJ: Princeton University Press, 2008), 287–91.
28 Wolin, *Democracy Incorporated*, 276–8, 290.
29 Wolin, "Fugitive Democracy," 31, 37–9, 42–3.
30 This draws from an analysis of Laclau's theory in Robert L. Ivie and Oscar Giner, "A Democratic People's Dissent from War," *Javnost–The Public*, 24, no. 3 (2017): 202–4. Our essay's discussion of Laclau relies primarily on two of his books: Ernesto Laclau, *On Populist Reason* (London: Verso, 2005) and Ernesto Laclau, *The Rhetorical Foundations of Society* (London: Verso, 2014).
31 Laclau, *Rhetorical Foundations*, 202–3. Emphasis in original.
32 Robert L. Ivie, "Democratic Spaces of Interdependence," *China Media Research* 13, no. 4 (2017): 17–27.
33 Kitri Sharma, *Interdependence: Biology and Beyond* (New York: Fordham University Press, 2015), 2, 15–16, 100–1.
34 Kenneth Burke, *A Grammar of Motives* (1945; Berkeley: University of California Press, 1969), 507–9.
35 Anthony J. Marsella, "The United States of America: 'A Culture of War,'" *International Journal of Intercultural Relations*, 35, no. 6 (2011): 714–28.
36 Black Lives Matter, "This is Murder," George Floyd Death, Full Video, May 28, 2020, https://www.youtube.com/watch?v=iE0M7ECBRno. Floyd was a black man killed on May 25, 2020 by Derek Chauvin, a white police officer, after being arrested for allegedly using a counterfeit bill. Floyd was handcuffed and lying face down on the street next to a police

vehicle while Officer Chauvin kneeled on his neck for over eight minutes and other officers kept bystanders from intervening. Floyd's last words were "I can't breathe."

37 Martin Luther King, Jr., "Beyond Vietnam: A Time to Break Silence," April 4, 1967, *American Rhetoric Online Speech Bank*, https://www.americanrhetoric.com/speechbank.htm.

38 Howard Zinn, *A People's History of the United States* (New York: Perennial, 2001); Howard Zinn, *Just War* (Milan: Charta, 2005), 46; Howard Zinn, *Passionate Declarations: Essays for War and Justice* (New York: Perennial, 2003), 56.

39 See Ivie and Giner, "Democratic People's Dissent," 209, 212.

40 A. J. Marsella, "A Culture of War," 714–28; Lene Hansen, *Security as Practice: Discourse Analysis and the Bosnian War* (New York: Routledge, 2006), 21–3; Robert L. Ivie, "Hierarchies of Equality: Positive Peace in a Democratic Idiom," in *The Handbook of Communication Ethics*, ed. George Cheney, Steve May, and Debashish Munshi (New York: Routledge, 2011), 377–9.

41 Robert L. Ivie, "Enabling Democratic Dissent," *Quarterly Journal of Speech* 101, no. 1 (2015): 50–1.

42 Howard Zinn, *A Power Governments Cannot Suppress* (San Francisco, CA: City Lights Publishers, 2007), 270. This quote appeared in multiple books and articles written by Zinn, including his autobiography, *You Can't Be Neutral on a Moving Train: A Personal History of Our Times* (Boston: Beacon, 1994).

43 Howard Zinn, *Just War* (Milano, Italy: Charta, 2005), 25, 27.

44 Howard Zinn, *Passionate Declarations*, 80.

45 Zinn, *Passionate Declarations*, 85–7.

46 Zinn, *Passionate Declarations*, 87–9.

47 Zinn, *Passionate Declarations*, 83.

48 Zinn, *Passionate Declarations*, 91–2.

49 Zinn, *Passionate Declarations*, 96.

50 Zinn, *Passionate Declarations*, 99.

51 Zinn, *Passionate Declarations*, 104.

52 Zinn, *Just War*, 37.

53 Zinn, *Just War*, 48.

54 Howard Zinn, "The Bombing of Royan," in *Howard Zinn on War* (New York: Seven Stories Press, 2001), 106, 107, 115, 120.

55 Zinn, "The Bombing of Royan," 115–6.

56 Zinn, "One Iraqi's Story," in *Howard Zinn on War*, 33–4.

57 Zinn, "Bombing Iraq," in *Howard Zinn on War*, 40.

58 Zinn, *Just War*, 13–4, 56–7.

59 Zinn, *Just War*, 19.

60 Zinn, *Just War*, 15, 18–19.

61 Zinn, "If History is to be Creative," in *A Power Governments Cannot Suppress*, 11–12, 15.

62 Zinn explained his purpose in his edited volume of dramatic readings celebrating the enduring spirit of dissent: "I prefer to try to tell the story of the discovery of America from the viewpoint of the Arawaks, of the Constitution from the standpoint of the slaves, of the rise of industrialism as seen by the young women in the Lowell textile mills, the conquest

of the Philippines as seen by Black soldiers on Luzon, the postwar American empire as seen by peons in Latin America." Howard Zinn, ed., *The People Speak: American Voices, Some Famous, Some Little Known* (New York: HarperCollins, 2004), 1–2. For a broad collection of dissenting voices, see Howard Zinn and Anthony Arnove, *Voices of a People's History of the United States* (New York: Seven Stories Press, 2004). For the story Zinn told to represent these absented voices, see Howard Zinn, *A People's History of the United States*.

63 Zinn, "Unsung Heroes," in *A Power Governments Cannot Suppress*, 60, 61.
64 Zinn, "Henry David Thoreau," in *A Power Governments Cannot Suppress*, 132.
65 Zinn, "Nationalism," in *A Power Governments Cannot Suppress*, 146, 152, 154.
66 Zinn, "Governments Lie," in *A Power Governments Cannot Suppress*, 200–1, 205.
67 Zinn, "The Optimism of Uncertainty," in *A Power Governments Cannot Suppress*, 267, 270.

SELECTED BIBLIOGRAPHY

Aeschylus. *Aeschylus I: Oresteia*. Translated by Richmond Lattimore. Chicago: University of Chicago Press, 1953.
———. *Prometheus Bound*. Translated by James Scully and C. John Herington. Oxford: University Press, 1975.
———. "The Oresteia." In *The Complete Aeschylus*, vol. 1, edited by Peter Burian and Alan Shapiro. Oxford: University Press, 2011.
Agreda, Venerable Mary of. *The Mystical City of God: Popular Abridgment of the Divine History and Life of the Virgin Mother of God*. Translated by Fiscar Marison. Rockford, IL: Tan Books and Publishers, 1978.
Aguinaga, Carlos Blanco, Julio Rodríguez Puértolas, and Iris Zavala. *Historia Social de la Literatura Española (en Lengua Castellana)*. 3 vols. Madrid: Editorial Castalia, 1979.
Anderson, Fred, and Andrew Cayton. *The Dominion of War: Empire and Liberty in North America, 1500–2000*. New York: Viking, 2005.
Andrejevic, Mark. "The *Jouissance* of Trump." *Television & New Media* 17, no. 7 (2016): 651–5.
Appel, Edward C. "Burlesque, Tragedy, and a (Potentially) 'Yuuuge' 'Breaking of a Frame': Donald Trump's Rhetoric as 'Early Warning'?" *Communication Quarterly* 66, no. 2 (2018): 157–75.
Aristophanes. *The Birds*. Translated by William Arrowsmith. New York: Mentor Books, 1970.
———. *The Clouds*. Translated by William Arrowsmith. New York: Mentor Books, 1970.
Aristotle. *Poetics*. Translated by Gerald Else. Ann Arbor, MI: University of Michigan Press, 1973.

Arnott, Peter. "Later Tragedy: Euripides and the Medea." In *An Introduction to the Greek Theatre*, 90–118. Bloomington: Indiana University Press, 1967.

Arrom, José Juan. *Hispanoamérica: Panorama Contemporáneo de su Cultura*. New York: Harper and Row, 1969.

Arrowsmith, William. "Aristophanes' Birds: The Fantasy Politics of Eros." *Arion: A Journal of Humanities and the Classics*. New Series, 1, no. 1 (1973): 119–67.

———. "Editor's Foreword." In *Prometheus Bound*, edited by Aeschylus, translated by James Scully and C. John Herington, v–x. Oxford: University Press, 1975.

———. "Introduction." In *The Clouds*, edited by Aristophanes, translated by William Arrowsmith, 7–16. New York: Mentor Books, 1970.

———. "Introduction." In *Alcestis*, edited by Euripides, translated by William Arrowsmith. New York: Oxford University Press, 1989.

Bacevich, Andrew J. *American Empire*. Cambridge, MA: Harvard University Press, 2002.

———. *The Limits of Power: The End of American Exceptionalism*. New York: Henry Holt and Company, 2008.

———. *The New American Militarism: How Americans Are Seduced by War*. New York: Oxford University Press, 2005.

Beckett, Samuel. *Happy Days*. New York: Grove Press, 1989.

Beissel, Stephen. *Fra Angelico*. New York: Parkstone Press, 2007.

Bell, Madison Smart. *Toussaint Louverture*. New York: Pantheon Books, 2007.

Berghe, Kristine Vanden. "The Forgotten Caliban of Aníbal Ponce." In *Constellation Caliban: Figurations of a Character*, edited by Nadia Lie and Theo D'haen, 185–98. Amsterdam: Editions Rodópi, 1997.

Bird, Robert Montgomery. "The Gladiator." In *Early American Drama*, edited by Jeffrey H. Richards, 166–242. 1831; New York: Penguin Books, 1997.

Bloom, Harold, ed. *Bloom's BioCritiques: Emily Dickinson*. Broomall, PA: Chelsea House Publishers, 2003.

Borges, Jorge Luis. "A History of Angels." In *Selected Non-fictions*, edited by Eliot Weinberger and translated by Esther Allen, Suzanne Jill Levine and Eliot Weinberger, 16–19. 1926; New York: Penguin Books, 2000.

———. *This Craft of Verse*. Cambridge: Harvard University Press, 2000.

Boulding, Elise. *Cultures of Peace: The Hidden Side of History*. Syracuse, NY: Syracuse University Press, 2000.

Brecht, Bertolt. "Study of the First Scene of Shakespeare's *Coriolanus*." In *Brecht on Theatre: The Development of an Aesthetic*, edited and translated by John Willett, 252–65. New York: Hill and Wang, 1986.

———. "Writing the Truth: Five Difficulties." In *Galileo*, edited by Eric Bentley and translated by Charles Laughton, 131–50. New York: Grove Press, 1966.

Bright, William. *A Coyote Reader*. Berkeley, CA: University of California Press, 1993.

Bringhurst, Robert. *The Tree of Meaning: Language, Mind and Ecology*. Berkeley: Counterpoint, 2008.

Brock, Peter. "Gandhi's Nonviolence and His War Service." *Peace & Change* 7, no. 1–2 (1981): 71–84.

SELECTED BIBLIOGRAPHY

Burke, Kenneth. *A Grammar of Motives*. 1945; Berkeley, CA: University of California Press, 1969.

———. *A Rhetoric of Motives*. 1950; Berkeley, CA: University of California Press, 1969.

———. *Attitudes Toward History*, 3rd ed. Berkeley: University of California Press, 1984.

———. *Language as Symbolic Action: Essays on Life, Literature, and Method*. Berkeley: University of California Press, 1966.

———. *Permanence and Change*, 3rd ed. Berkeley, CA: University of California Press, 1984.

———. *The Rhetoric of Religion*. Berkeley: University of California Press, 1970.

Butterworth, Michael. *Baseball and Rhetorics of Purity: The National Pastime and American Identity During the War on Terror*. Tuscaloosa: University of Alabama Press, 2010.

Cady, Duane. *From Warism to Pacifism: A Moral Continuum*. Philadelphia: Temple University Press, 1989.

Calabrese, Andrew. "Liberalism's Disease: Civility Above Justice." *European Journal of Communication* 30, no. 5 (2015): 539–53.

Campbell, David. *Writing Security: United States Foreign Policy and the Politics of Identity*. Rev. ed. Minneapolis: University of Minnesota Press, 1998.

Campbell, Joseph. *The Hero with a Thousand Faces*, 2nd ed. Princeton, NJ: Princeton University Press, 1968.

———. *The Inner Reaches of Outer Space*. 1986; Novato, CA: New World Library, 2002.

———. *The Masks of God*. 4 vols. New York: Penguin Books, 1968.

Camus, Albert. *The Fall*. 1956; New York: Vintage Books, 1991.

Carpenter, F. B. *Six Months at the White House with Lincoln: The Story of a Picture*. 1866; Watkins Glen, NY: Century House, 1961.

Cawley, A. C., ed. *Everyman and Medieval Miracle Plays*. 1956; New York: Everyman's Library, 1967.

Certeau, Michel de. *The Capture of Speech and Other Political Writings*. Edited by Luce Giard and translated by Tom Conley. Minneapolis: University of Minnesota Press, 1997.

———. *The Practice of Everyday Life*. Translated by Steen Rendall. Berkeley: University of California Press, 1984.

Césaire, Aimé. *A Tempest*. Translated by Richard Miller. New York: Ubu Repertory Theatre Publications, 1992.

———. *Notebook of a Return to the Native Land*. Translated by Clayton Eshleman and Annette Smith. 1939; Middletown, CT: Wesleyan University Press, 2001.

Chappell, Paul. *Peaceful Revolution*. Westport, CT: Easton Studio Press, 2012.

———. *The Art of Waging Peace*. Westport, CT: Prospecta Press, 2013.

———. *Will War Ever End?* Weston, CT: Ashoka Books, 2009.

Cherniavsky, Eva. *Neocitizenship: Political Culture After Democracy*. New York: New York University Press, 2017.

Chernus, Ira. "Franklin D. Roosevelt's Narrative of National Insecurity." *Journal of Multicultural Discourses* 11, no. 2 (2016): 135–48.

———. *Monsters to Destroy: The Neoconservative War on Terror and Sin*. Boulder, CO: Paradigm, 2006.

Cortright, David. *Peace: A History of Movements and Ideas*. Cambridge: Cambridge University Press, 2008.

Daniel, Stephen H. *Myth and Modern Philosophy*. Philadelphia: Temple University Press, 1990.

Darsey, James. *The Prophetic Tradition and Radical Rhetoric in America*. New York: New York University Press, 1997.

de Jesús, Santa Teresa. *Su Vida*. 1565; Madrid: Colección Austral, 1980.

de la Cruz, Sor Juana Inés. *The Answer/La Respuesta, Including a Selection of Poems*. Edited and translated by Electa Arenal and Amanda Powell. New York: Feminist Press at the City University of New York, 1994.

Deer, Patrick. "Mapping Contemporary American War Culture." *College Literature* 43, no. 1 (2016): 48–90.

Deloria, Vine. *Custer Died for Your Sins: An Indian Manifesto*. Norman: University of Oklahoma Press, 1988.

Denton-Borhaug, Kelly. *And Then Your Soul Is Gone: Moral Injury and U.S. War Culture*. Oakville, CT: Equinox, 2021.

———. *U.S. War-Culture, Sacrifice and Salvation*. Oakville, CT: Equinox, 2011.

Dickinson, Emily. *The Complete Poems of Emily Dickinson*. Edited by Thomas H. Johnson. New York: Back Bay Books, 1976.

———. *The Poems of Emily Dickinson*. Edited by R. W. Franklin. 1999; Cambridge: Harvard University Press, 2005.

Dilliplane, Susanna. "Race, Rhetoric, and Running for President: Unpacking the Significance of Barack Obama's 'A More Perfect Union' Speech." *Rhetoric & Public Affairs* 15, no. 1 (2012): 127–52.

Donaldson, Ian. *Ben Jonson: A Life*. New York: Oxford University Press, 2011.

Doty, William G. *Myth: A Handbook*. Tuscaloosa, AL: University of Alabama Press, 2004.

———. *Mythography: The Study of Myths and Rituals*, 2nd ed. Tuscaloosa, AL: University of Alabama Press, 2000.

Dow, Bonnie. "Taking Trump Seriously: Persona and Presidential Politics in 2016." *Women's Studies in Communication* 40, no. 2 (2017): 136–9.

Dubois, Laurent and John D. Garrigus, eds. *Slave Revolution in the Caribbean, 1789–1904: A Brief History with Documents*. New York: Palgrave Macmillan, 2006.

Dyson, Michael Eric. "Foreword." In *White Fragility: Why It's So Hard for White People to Talk about Racism*, edited by Robin Diangelo, ix–xii. Boston: Beacon Press, 2018.

Edwards, Jason A. "Make America Great Again: Donald Trump and Redefining the U.S. Role in the World." *Communication Quarterly* 66, no. 2 (2018): 176–95.

Ehrenreich, Barbara. *Blood Rites: Origins and History of the Passions of War*. New York: Henry Holt and Company, 1997.

Eliot, T. S. "The Fire Storm." In *Collected Poems 1909–1962*, 60–4. 1922; New York: Harcourt Brace Jovanovich, 1971.

Elliott, Michael A. *Custerology: The Enduring Legacy of the Indian Wars and George Armstrong Custer*. Chicago: Lakeside Press, 2004.

Engels, Jeremy. *Enemyship: Democracy and Counter-Revolution in the Early Republic*. East Lansing: Michigan State University Press, 2010.

Englehardt, Tom. *The American Way of War: How Bush's Wars Became Obama's*. Chicago: Haymarket Books, 2010.

———. *The End of Victory Culture: Cold War America and the Disillusioning of a Generation*. New York: Basic Books, 1995.

Erdoes, Richard, and Alfoso Ortiz, eds. *American Indian Trickster Tales*. New York: Penguin Books, 1998.

Euripides. *Alcestis*. Translated by William Arrowsmith. Oxford: Oxford University Press, 1974.

———. *Iphigeneia at Aulis*. Translated by W. S. Merwin and George E. Dimock, Jr. New York: Oxford University Press, 1978.

———. *Iphigeneia in Tauris*. Translated by Richmond Lattimore. New York: Oxford University Press, 1973.

Fanon, Frantz. *The Wretched of the Earth*. New York: Grove Press, 1963.

Fast, Howard. *Spartacus*. 1951; New York: Bantam Books, 1960.

Faust, Drew Gilpin. *This Republic of Suffering: Death and the American Civil War*. New York: Alfred A. Knopf, 2008.

Feffer, John. *Splinterlands*. Chicago: Haymarket Books, 2016.

Ferguson, R. Brian. "Archaeology, Cultural Anthropology, and the Origins and Intensification of War." In *The Archaeology of Warfare: Prehistories of Raiding and Conquest*, edited by Elizabeth N. Arkush and Mark W. Allen, 469–523. Gainesville: University Press of Florida, 2006.

———. "Ten Points on War." *Social Analysis* 52, no. 2 (2008): 32–49.

Fernández Retamar, Roberto. *Caliban and Other Essays*. Minneapolis: University of Minnesota Press, 1989.

Ferner, Mike. *Inside the Red Zone: A Veteran for Peace Reports from Iraq*. Westport, CT: Praeger, 2006.

Fiala, Andrew. *The Just War Myth: The Moral Illusions of War*. Lanham, MD: Rowman & Littlefield, 2008.

Frentz, Thomas S. and Janice Hocker Rushing. "Integrating Ideology and Archetype in Rhetorical Criticism, Part II: A Case Study of *Jaws*." *Quarterly Journal of Speech* 79, no. 1 (1993): 61–81.

Fry, Douglas. *The Human Potential for Peace: An Anthropological Challenge to Assumptions about War and Violence*. New York: Oxford University Press, 2006.

Frye, Northrop. *Anatomy of Criticism*. Princeton, NJ: Princeton University Press, 1957.

Fuchs, Christian. "Authoritarian Capitalism, Authoritarian Movements and Authoritarian Communication." *Media, Culture & Society* 40, no. 5 (2018): 779–91.

Gallup, Donald C. *Eugene O'Neill and His Eleven-Play Cycle: "A Tale of Possessors Self-Dispossessed."* New Haven: Yale University Press, 1998.

Galton, Francis. *Inquiries into Human Faculty and Its Development*. London: Blurb, 2019.

García Lorca, Federico. "San Gabriel (Sevilla)." In *Obras Completas*, vol. 1, 414–16. 1924–7; Madrid: Aguilar, 1980.

———. "Teoría y Juego del Duende." In *Obras Completas*, vol. 1, 1097–1109. Madrid: Aguilar, 1980.

Gelpí, Juan G. *Literatura y Paternalismo en Puerto Rico*. San Juan: Editorial Universidad de Puerto Rico, 1994.

Genesio, Jerry. *Veterans for Peace: The First Decade*. Falmouth, ME: Pequawket Press, 1997.

Gerbaudo, Paolo. *The Mask and the Flag: Populism, Citizenism and Global Protest*. London: Hurst & Company, 2017.

Gibson, Ian. *Luis Buñuel: La Forja de un Cineasta Universal 1900–1938*. Barcelona: Penguin Random House Grupo Editorial, 2015.

Gilman, Richard. *Common and Uncommon Masks*. New York: Vintage Books, 1972.

———. *Decadence: The Strange Life of an Epithet*. New York: Farrar, Straus, and Giroux, 1979.

Gilmore, Jason, Penelope Sheets, and Charles Rowling. "Make No Exceptions Save One: American Exceptionalism, the American Presidency, and the Age of Obama." *Communication Monographs* 83, no. 4 (2016): 505–20.

Giner, Oscar. "Exorcisms." *Theater* 9, no. 3 (1978): 75–81.

———. "Portraits of Rebellion: Geronimo's Portrait of 1884." In *Rhetoric, Materiality and Politics*, edited by Barbara Biesecker and John Lucaites, 277–92. New York: Peter Lang, 2009.

———. "Rabinal Achí," *Tyuony 2*, Santa Fe: Institute of American Indian Arts, 1986.

———. "The Death of Marlon Brando." *Communication and Critical/Cultural Studies* 2, no. 2 (2005): 83–106.

Giroux, Henry A. "War Culture and the Politics of Violence." *Symplokē* 25, no. 1–2 (2017): 191–218.

Glantz, Aaron. *Winter Soldier, Iraq and Afghanistan: Eyewitness Accounts of the Occupation*. Chicago: Haymarket Books, 2008.

Goodwin, Doris Kearns. *Team of Rivals: The Political Genius of Abraham Lincoln*. New York: Simon and Schuster, 2005.

Goodwyn, Lawrence. *Democratic Promise: The Populist Moment in America*. New York: Oxford University Press, 1976.

Grant, Ulysses S. *Personal Memoirs*. 1885; New York: Penguin Classics, 1999.

Guterl, Matthew. *American Mediterranean: Southern Slaveholders in the Age of Emancipation*. Cambridge, MA: Harvard University Press, 2008.

Habbegger, Alfred. *My Wars Are Laid Away in Books: The Life of Emily Dickinson*. New York: Random House, 2001.

Hansen, Lene. *Security as Practice: Discourse Analysis and the Bosnian War*. London: Routledge, 2006.

Hartnett, Stephen John, and Laura Ann Stengrim. *Globalization and Empire: The U.S. Invasion of Iraq, Free Markets, and the Twilight of Democracy*. Tuscaloosa: University of Alabama Press, 2006.

Hasian, Marouf. *Drone Warfare and Lawfare in a Post-Heroic Age*. Tuscaloosa: University of Alabama Press, 2016.

Hasian, Marouf Arif, Jr., and Megan D. McFarlane. *Cultural Rhetorics of American Exceptionalism and the Bin Laden Raid*. New York: Peter Lang, 2013.

Hasian, Marouf Arif, Jr., Shawn Lawson, and Megan D. McFarlane. *The Rhetorical Invention of America's National Security State*. Lanham, MD: Lexington Books, 2015.

Hayes, Heather Ashley. *Violent Subjects and Rhetorical Cartography in the Age of the Terror Wars.* New York: Palgrave Macmillan, 2016.
Hearn, Alison. "Trump's 'Reality' Hustle." *Television & New Media* 17, no. 7 (2016): 656–9.
Heidt, Stephen J. *Resowing the Seeds of War: Presidential Peace Rhetoric since 1945.* East Lansing: Michigan State University Press, 2021.
Henderson, Archibald. *George Bernard Shaw: Man of the Century.* New York: Appleton-Century Crofts, 1956.
Hernandez, José. *El Gaucho Martín Fierro y La Vuelta de Martín Fierro.* Madrid: Edicones Castalia, 2001.
Hersey, John. *Hiroshima.* 1946; New York: Bantam Books, 1968.
Hodges, Adam, ed. *Discourses of War and Peace.* New York: Oxford University Press, 2013.
Hughes, Richard T. *Myths America Lives By.* Urbana: University of Illinois Press, 2003.
Hyde, Lewis. *Trickster Makes This World.* New York: North Point Press, 1999.
Hynes, William J., and William G. Doty, eds. *Mythical Trickster Figures: Contours, Contexts, and Criticisms.* Tuscaloosa, AL: University of Alabama Press, 1993.
Ionesco, Eugene. *Exit the King.* New York: Grove Press, 1963.
Isaac, Jeffrey C. *#AgainstTrump: Notes from Year One.* New York: Public Seminar Books, 2018.
Ivie, Robert L. *Democracy and America's War on Terror.* Tuscaloosa: University of Alabama Press, 2005.
———. "Democracy and Militarism." In *The Marketing of War in the Age of Neo-Militarism,* edited by Kostas Gouliamos and Christos Kassimeris, 97–106. New York: Routledge, 2012.
———. "Depolarizing the Discourse of American Security: Constitutive Properties of Positive Peace in Barack Obama's Rhetoric of Change." In *Philosophy After Hiroshima,* edited by Edward Demenchonok, 233–61. Newcastle upon Tyne: Cambridge Scholars Publishing, 2010.
———. *Dissent from War.* Bloomfield, CT: Kumarian Press, 2007.
———. "Dissenting Democratically from Trump's Toxic Tropes." *Javnost–The Public* 30, no. 1 (2023): 1–17.
———. "Enabling Democratic Dissent." *Quarterly Journal of Speech* 101, no. 1 (2015): 46–59.
———. "Hierarchies of Equality: Positive Peace in a Democratic Idiom." In *Handbook of Communication Ethics,* edited by George Cheney, Steve May, and Debashish Munshi, 374–86. New York: Rutledge, 2011.
———. "Kenneth Burke's Attitude Toward Rhetoric." *Rhetorica Scandinavica* 73 (June 2016): 13–29.
———. "Obama at West Point: A Study in Ambiguity of Purpose." *Rhetoric & Public Affairs* 14, no. 4 (2011): 727–59.
———. "Productive Criticism at the Crossroads: Interventions, Trajectories, and Intersections." *Review of Communication* 16, no. 1 (2016): 104–7.
———. "Productive Criticism Then and Now." *American Communication Journal* 4, no. 3 (2001). http://ac-journal.org/journal/vol4/iss3/special/ivie.htm.
———. "Rhetorical Aftershocks of Trump's Ascendency: Salvation by Demolition and Deal Making." *Res Rhetorica* 4, no. 2 (2017): 61–79.

Ivie, Robert L., and Oscar Giner. "American Exceptionalism in a Democratic Idiom: Transacting the Mythos of Change in the 2008 Presidential Campaign." *Communication Studies* 60, no. 4 (2009): 359–75.

———. *Hunt the Devil: A Demonology of US War Culture*. Tuscaloosa: University of Alabama Press, 2015.

———. "More Good, Less Evil: Contesting the Mythos of National Insecurity in the 2008 Presidential Primaries." *Rhetoric & Public Affairs* 12, no. 2 (2009): 279–301.

Jackson, Helen. *A Century of Dishonor: A Sketch of the United States Government Dealings with Some of the Indian Tribes*. 1881; New York: Barnes and Noble, 1994.

Johnson, Chalmers. *The Sorrows of Empire: Militarism, Secrecy, and the End of the Republic*. New York: Metropolitan Books, 2004.

Joyce, James. *A Portrait of the Artist as a Young Man*. 1916; New York: Penguin Books, 1993.

Judis, John B. *The Populist Explosion: How the Great Recession Transformed American and European Politics*. New York: Columbia Global Reports, 2016.

Jung, Carl. "The Archetypes and the Collective Unconsious." In *Collected Works of C.G. Jung*, vol. 9 (Part 1). Princeton, NJ: Princeton University Press, 1969.

———. "The Structure of the Psyche." In *The Portable Jung*, edited by Joseph Campbell, 23–46. New York: Penguin Books, 1976.

Kazin, Michael. *The Populist Persuasion: An American History*. Rev. ed. Ithaca, NY: Cornell University Press, 1998.

Keckley, Elizabeth. *Behind the Scenes. Or, Thirty Years a Slave, and Four Years in the White House*. 1868; Oxford: University Press, 1988.

Kennedy, Sheila. *God and Country: America in Red and Blue*. Waco, TX: Baylor University Press, 2007.

Kierkegaard, Soren. *Fear and Trembling*. London: Penguin Books, 2003.

Kopit, Arthur. *Indians*. New York: Bantam Books, 1971.

Kumar, Deepa. "National Security Culture: Gender, Race, and Class in the Production of Imperial Citizenship." *International Journal of Communication* 11 (2017): 2154–77.

Kushner, Tony. *Angels in America Part Two: Perestroika*. New York: Theatre Communications Group, 1996.

———. *Lincoln: The Screenplay*. New York: Theatre Communications Group, 2012.

Laclau, Ernesto. *On Populist Reason*. London: Verso, 2005.

———. *The Rhetorical Foundations of Society*. London: Verso, 2014.

Laclau, Ernesto, and Chantal Mouffe. *Hegemony and Socialist Strategy: Towards a Radical Democratic Politics*, 2nd ed. London: Verso, 2001.

Larana, Enrique, Hank Johnston, and Joseph R. Gusfield, eds. *New Social Movements: From Ideology to Identity*, Rev. ed. Philadelphia: Temple University Press, 1994.

Las Casas, Bartolomé de. *A Short Account of the Destruction of the Indies*. New York: Penguin Books, 1992.

Lawrence, D. H. *Studies in Classic American Literature*. Garden City, NY: Doubleday and Co., 1955.

Lazarus, Edward. *Black Hills and White Justice: The Sioux Nation versus the United States, 1775 to the Present*. New York: Harper Collins, 1991.

Lederach, John Paul. *The Moral Imagination: The Art and Soul of Building Peace*. New York: Oxford University Press, 2005.
Lederer, William J., and Eugene Burdick. *The Ugly American*. 1956; New York: W. W. Norton, 1999.
Leeming, David Adams. *The World of Myth*. New York: Oxford University Press, 1990.
Levinson, Nan. *War Is Not a Game: The New Antiwar Soldiers and the Movement They Built*. New Brunswick, NJ: Rutgers University Press, 2014.
Levitsky, Steven, and Daniel Ziblatt. *How Democracies Die*. New York: Penguin Random House, 2018.
Lifton, Robert J., and Greg Mitchell. *Hiroshima in America: A Half Century of Denial*. New York: Avon Books, 1995.
Lincoln, Abraham. *Speeches and Writings, 1859–1865*. Edited by Don E. Fehrenbaher. New York: Library of America, 1989.
———. *The Portable Abraham Lincoln*. Edited by Andrew Delbanco. New York: Penguin Books, 1993.
Liu, Changming. "US War Culture and the Destiny of the Empire." *International Critical Thought* 12, no. 3 (2022): 370–98.
Longfellow, Henry Wadsworth. *The Complete Poetical Works of Henry Wadsworth Longfellow*. Cutchogue, NY: Buccaneer Books, 1993.
Lopes, Sal, ed. *The Wall: Images and Offerings from the Vietnam Veterans Memorial*. New York: Collins Publisher, 1987.
Lukacs, John. *Democracy and Populism: Fear and Hatred*. New Haven, CT: Yale University Press, 2005.
———. *A Short History of the Twentieth Century*. Cambridge, MA: Harvard University Press, 2013.
Mails, Thomas E. *The Mystic Warriors of the Plains*. New York: Barnes and Noble, 1995.
Mali, Joseph. *The Rehabilitation of Myth: Vico's "New Science."* Cambridge, UK: Cambridge University Press, 1992.
Marlowe, Christopher. *Doctor Faustus: The 1604-Version Edition*. Edited by Michael Keefer. Ontario: Broadview Press, 1995.
Marqués, René. *Sacrificio en el Monte Moriah*. San Juan: Editorial Antillana, 1969.
Marsella, Anthony J. "The United States of America: 'A Culture of War.'" *International Journal of International Relations* 35, no. 6 (2011): 714–28.
Martí, José. *La Edad de Oro*. 1889; México: Fondo de Cultura Económica, 1995.
———. *Obras completas*. 28 vols. La Habana: Editorial Nacional de Cuba, 1963.
———. *Selected Writings*. Edited and translated by Esther Allen. New York: Penguin Books, 2002.
Masters, Edgar Lee, ed. "Harry Wilmans." In *Spoon River Anthology*, 197–8. 1915; New York: Macmillan Publishing, 1978.
Meacham, Jon. *The Soul of America: The Battle for Our Better Angels*. New York: Random House, 2018.
Mencken, H. L. *Prejudices: First, Second, and Third Series*. New York: The Library of America, 2010.

Merceica, Jennifer R. "Dangerous Demagogues and Weaponized Communication." *Rhetoric Society Quarterly* 49, no. 3 (2019): 264–79.

———. *Founding Fictions*. Tuscaloosa: University of Alabama Press, 2010.

Merton, Thomas. *A Search for Solitude: The Journals of Thomas Merton*. Edited by Lawrence S. Cunningham, vol. 3. 1952–60; San Francisco: HarperSanFrancisco, 1996.

———. *Entering the Silence: Becoming a Monk and Writer (The Journals of Thomas Merton)*. Edited by Jonathan Montaldo, vol. 2. 1941–52; New York: HarperCollins, 1995.

Messner, Michael A. *Unconventional Combat: Intersectional Action in the Veterans' Peace Movement*. New York: Oxford University Press, 2021.

Miller, Arthur. *After the Fall*. New York: The Viking Press, 1964.

Moliere. *Don Juan*. Translated by Richard Wilbur. New York: Harcourt, 2001.

Monegal, Emir Rodríguez, ed., *The Borzoi Anthology of Latin American Literature*. New York: Alfred A. Knopf, 1977.

Morfi, Angelina. *Historia Crítica de un Siglo de Teatro Puertorriqueño*. San Juan: Instituto de Cultura Puertorriqueña, 1980.

Mouffe, Chantal. *The Democratic Paradox*. London: Verso, 2000.

———. *The Return of the Political*. London: Verso, 1993.

Nadal, Rafael Martínez. "Introducción." In *El Público y Comedia Sin Título: Dos Obras Póstumas*, edited by Federico García Lorca. Barcelona: Editorial Seix Barral, 1978.

Nagler, A. M. *The Medieval Religious Stage: Shapes and Phantoms*. New Haven: Yale University Press, 1976.

Neihardt, John. *Black Elk Speaks*. Lincoln: University of Nebraska Press, 2004.

Nelson, John S. *Tropes of Politics: Science Theory, Rhetoric, Action*. Madison: University of Wisconsin Press, 1998.

Nietzsche, Friedrich. "On Truth and Lies in a Nonmoral Sense." In *Philosophy and Truth: Selections from Nietzsche's Notebooks of the Early 1870's*, edited and translated by Daniel Breazeale, 79–97. Amherst, NY: Humanity Books, 1999.

Obama, Barack. *Dreams from My Father: A Story of Race and Inheritance*. New York: Random House, 2004.

Ober, Josiah. *Demopolis: Democracy Before Liberalism in Theory and Practice*. New York: Cambridge University Press, 2017.

Ohr, Jessy J. "In Pursuit of Light War in Libya: *Kairotic* Justification of War that Just Happened." *Rhetoric & Public Affairs* 20, no. 2 (2017): 195–222.

O'Neill, Eugene. *The Plays of Eugene O'Neill*. 3 vols. New York: Random House, 1954.

Ortiz, Simon. *Shaking the Pumpkin*. Edited by Jerome Rothenberg. Albuquerque: University of New Mexico Press, 1991.

Orwell, George. "Politics and the English Language." In *Marxism and Art*, edited by Berel Lang and Forrest Williams, 426–37. 1946; New York: David McKay Company, 1972.

Osborn, Michael M. *Michael Osborn on Metaphor and Style*. East Lansing: Michigan State University Press, 2018.

———. "The Evolution of the Archetypal Sea in Rhetoric and Poetic." *Quarterly Journal of Speech* 63, no. 4 (1977): 347–63.

SELECTED BIBLIOGRAPHY

Ott, Brian L. "The Age of Twitter: Donald J. Trump and the Politics of Debasement." *Critical Studies in Media Communication* 34, no. 1 (2017): 59–68.

Pagels, Elaine. *The Origin of Satan*. New York: Random House, 1995.

Pané, Fray Ramón. *An Account of the Antiquities of the Indians*. Durham, NC: Duke University Press, 1999.

Parker, Alexander A. *The Allegorical Drama of Calderón*. 1943; Oxford: Dolphin Book Co., 1968.

Pease, Donald E. *The New American Exceptionalism*. Minneapolis: University of Minnesota Press, 2009.

Pham, Vincent M. "Our Foreign President Barack Obama: The Racial Logic of Birther Discourses." *Journal of International and Intercultural Communication* 8, no. 2 (2015): 86–107.

Phillips, Kendall R. "'The Safest Hands Are Our Own': Cinematic Affect, State Cruelty, and the Election of Donald J. Trump." *Communication and Critical/Cultural Studies* 15, no. 1 (2018): 85–9.

Pinker, Steven. *The Better Angels of Our Nature: Why Violence Has Declined*. New York: Viking, 2011.

Ponce, Aníbal. "Ariel o la Agonía de una Obstinada Ilusión." In *Obras*. La Habana: Casa de las Américas, 1975.

Postman, Neil. *Amusing Ourselves to Death: Public Discourse in the Age of Show Business*. New York: Viking, 1985.

Pound, Ezra. *ABC of Reading*. New York: New Directions, 1987.

Reeves, Joshua, and Matthew S. May. "The Peace Rhetoric of a War President: Barack Obama and the Just War Legacy." *Rhetoric & Public Affairs* 16, no. 4 (2013): 623–50.

Retamar, Roberto Fernández. "Caliban." In *Caliban and Other Essays*, translated by Lynn Garafola, David Arthur McMurray, and Roberto Márquez, 3–45. Minneapolis: University of Minnesota Press, 1989.

Ribadeneyra, Pedro de. *Vida de Ignacio de Loyola*. 1572; Madrid: Espasa-Calpe, 1967.

Ricciardi, Ramón and Bernardo Hurault, eds. *La Nueva Biblia Latinoamericana*. Madrid: Ediciones Paulinas, 1974.

Richards, Jeffrey H., ed. *Early American Drama*. New York: Penguin Books, 1997.

Roberts-Miller, Patricia. *Demagoguery and Democracy*. 2017; New York: The Experiment, LLC, 2020.

———. *Rhetoric and Demagoguery*. Carbondale: Southern Illinois University Press, 2019.

———. "The Mask of War and the War of Masks: The Fabricated Culture War Gets Deadly." *Javnost–The Public* 30, no. 1 (2023): 111–27.

Rodó, Enrique José. *Ariel*. Edited by Gordon Brotherston. Cambridge: University Press, 1967.

Rose, Martial, ed. *The Wakefield Mystery Plays*. New York: W. W. Norton & Co., 1969.

Rowland, Robert C. "Obama's Rhetoric of Myth and Reason." In *Reconsidering Obama: Reflections on Rhetoric*, edited by Robert E. Terrill, 51–68. New York: Peter Lang, 2017.

———. *The Rhetoric of Donald Trump: Nationalist Populism and American Democracy*. Lawrence: University of Kansas Press, 2021.

Rowland, Robert C., and John M. Jones. "One Dream: Barack Obama, Race, and the American Dream." *Rhetoric & Public Affairs* 14, no. 1 (2011): 125–54.

Rushing, Janice Hocker and Thomas S. Frentz. "Integrating Ideology and Archetype in Rhetorical Criticism." *Quarterly Journal of Speech* 77, no. 4 (1991): 385–406.

Schama, Simon. *Rough Crossings: Britain, the Slaves and the American Revolution.* New York: Harper Collins, 2006.

Shakespeare, William. *Coriolanus.* Edited by Reuben Brower. New York: Signet Classics, 1988.

———. *Hamlet, Prince of Denmark.* Edited by Philip Edwards. Cambridge: University Press, 2001.

———. *King Lear.* London: The Arden Shakespeare, 2003.

———. "Macbeth." In *The Yale Shakespeare,* edited by Wilbur L. Cross and Tucker Brooke. New York: Barnes & Noble, 1993.

———. "Othello." In *The Yale Shakespeare: The Complete Works,* edited by Wilbur L. Cross and Tucker Brooke. New York: Barnes & Noble, 1993.

———. "The Tempest." In *The Yale Shakespeare,* edited by Wilbur R. Cross and Tucker Brooke. New York: Barnes and Noble, 1993.

Sharma, Kriti. *Interdependence: Biology and Beyond.* Bronx, NY: Fordham University Press, 2015.

Shaw, George Bernard. *Buoyant Billions, Farfetched Fables and Shakes vs. Shav.* New York: Dodd, Mead and Co., 1951.

———. *Heartbreak House.* 1919; Baltimore, MD: Penguin Books, 1974.

———. *St. Joan.* New York: Viking Penguin, Inc., 1985.

Sherry, Michael S. *In the Shadow of War: The United States since the 1930s.* New Haven, CT: Yale University Press, 1995.

Shi-xu. "Cultural Discourse Studies." In *The International Encyclopedia of Language and Social Interaction,* edited by Karen Tracy, 288–97. Hoboken, NJ: John Wiley and Sons, Inc., 2015.

Simons, Jon and John Louis Lucaites, eds. *In/visible War: The Culture of War in Twenty-First-Century America.* New Brunswick, NJ: Rutgers University Press, 2017.

Skinnell, Ryan. "Using Democracy against Itself: Democratic Rhetoric as an Attack on Democratic Institutions." *Rhetoric Society Quarterly* 49, no. 3 (2019): 248–63.

Slotkin, Richard. *Gunfighter Nation: The Myth of the Frontier in Twentieth Century America.* Norman: University of Oklahoma Press, 1992.

———. *Regeneration Through Violence: The Mythology of the American Frontier, 1600–1860.* Norman: University of Oklahoma Press, 1973.

———. *The Fatal Environment: The Myth of the Frontier in the Age of Industrialization, 1800–1890.* Norman: University of Oklahoma Press, 1985.

Smith, Anna Marie. *Laclau and Mouffe: The Radical Democratic Imaginary.* London: Routledge, 1998.

Snyder, Tim. *On Tyranny: Twenty Lessons from the Twentieth Century.* New York: Tim Duggan Books, 2017.

Sophocles. *Oedipus the King.* Translated by Stephen Berg and Diskin Clay. New York: Oxford University Press, 1988.

Stahl, Roger. *Militainment, Inc.: War, Media, and Popular Culture.* New York: Routledge, 2010.

———. *Through the Crosshairs: War, Visual Culture, and the Weaponized Gaze.* Newark, NJ: Rutgers University Press, 2018.

Standish, Katerina, Heather Devere, Aden E. Suazo, and Rachel Rafferty, eds. *The Palgrave Handbook of Positive Peace*. Singapore: Palgrave Macmillan, 2022.

Steinbeck, John. *Zapata*. Edited by Robert Morsberger. New York: Penguin Books, 1993.

Stevenson, Robert Louis. *Dr. Jekyll and Mr. Hyde*. 1886; New York: Bantam Books, 1985.

Stuckey, Mary E. "American Elections and the Rhetoric of Political Change: Hyperbole, Anger, and Hope in U.S. Politics." *Rhetoric & Public Affairs* 20, no. 4 (2017): 667–94.

Tapia y Rivera, Alejandro. *Obras completas*. 3 vols. San Juan: Instituto de Cultura Puertorriqueña, 1968–70.

Terrill, Robert E. "An Uneasy Peace: Barack Obama's Nobel Peace Prize Lecture." *Rhetoric & Public Affairs* 14, no. 4 (2011): 761–79.

———. *Double-Consciousness and the Rhetoric of Barack Obama: The Price and Promise of Citizenship*. Columbia: University of South Carolina Press, 2015.

———. "The Post-Racial and Post-Ethical Discourse of Donald J. Trump." *Rhetoric & Public Affairs* 20, no. 3 (2017): 493–510.

Thomas, Hugh. *Cuba: The Pursuit of Freedom*. New York: Harper and Row, 1971.

———. *Rivers of Gold: The Rise of the Spanish Empire, from Columbus to Magellan*. New York: Random House, 2005.

Turner, Frederick Jackson. *The Frontier in American History*. New York: Holt, Rinehart & Winston, 1962.

Twain, Mark. *Collected Tales, Sketches, Speeches and Essays, 1891–1910*. Edited by Louis J. Budd. New York: Library of America, 1992.

———. *Roughing It*. New York: New American Library, 1962.

Utley, Robert. *The Last Days of the Sioux Nation*. New Haven: Yale University Press, 2004.

Vasconcelos, José. *La Raza Cósmica: Misión de la Raza Iberoamericana*. Madrid: Aguilar, 1966.

Vico, Giambattista. *New Science*. Translated by David Marsh. 1744; London: Penguin Books, 1999.

———. *On the Most Ancient Wisdom of the Italians*. Translated by L. M. Parker. 1710; London: Cornell University Press, 1988.

Vidal, Gore. *Lincoln: A Novel*. New York: Ballantine Books, 1984.

Walcott, Derek. *Complete Poems, 1948–1984*. New York: Farrar, Straus & Giroux, 2001.

Whitman, Walt. "Forrest as Gladiator." In *A Sourcebook in Theatrical History*, edited by A. M. Nagler, 545–46. 1846; New York: Dover Publications, 1952.

———. *Leaves of Grass: First and 'Death-Bed' Editions*. Edited by Karen Karbiener. 1891; New York: Barnes and Noble Classics, 2004.

Williams, William Carlos. *In the American Grain*. New York: New Directions, 1956.

Wilson, Peter Lamborn. *Angels*. New York: Pantheon Books, 1980.

Wolin, Sheldon S. *Democracy Incorporated*. Princeton, NJ: Princeton University Press, 2008.

———. *Politics and Vision: Continuity and Innovation in Western Political Thought*, expanded edition. Princeton, NJ: Princeton University Press, 2004.

Zappen, James P. "Kenneth Burke on Dialectical-Rhetorical Transcendence." *Philosophy and Rhetoric* 42, no. 3 (2009): 290–5.

Zinn, Howard. *A People's History of the United States*. New York: Perennial, 2001.

———. *A Power Governments Cannot Suppress*. San Francisco, CA: City Lights Publishers, 2007.

———. *Howard Zinn on War*. New York: Seven Stories Press, 2001.
———. *Just War*. Milano, Italy: Charta, 2005.
———. *Passionate Declarations: Essays on War and Justice*. New York: Perennial, 2003.
———, ed. *The People Speak: American Voices, Some Famous, Some Little Known*. New York: HarperCollins, 2004.
Zinn, Howard, and Anthony Arnove. *Voices of a People's History of the United States*. New York: Seven Stories Press, 2004.

NOTES ON AUTHORS

Oscar Giner is a Professor at the Herberger College of Design and the Arts at Arizona State University, Tempe. His research focuses on myths and rituals of the Spanish Religious stage and Native American performance practices. He has published book chapters in *Rhetoric, Materiality and Politics* (2009); with Robert L. Ivie in *Sourcebook for Political Communication Research* (2011); and in Carmelo Santana Mojica's edition of Tirso de Molina's *El burlador de Sevilla* (2010). He is coauthor, with Robert L. Ivie, of *Hunt the Devil: A Demonology of US War Culture* (2015). His artistic work extends to professional playwriting, translating, directing, and acting in venues ranging from Off-Broadway to San Juan, Puerto Rico.

Robert L. Ivie is Professor Emeritus in English (Rhetoric) and American Studies at Indiana University, Bloomington. His research focuses on political rhetoric and the critique of U.S. war culture with a particular interest in democratic discourse. He is co-author, with Oscar Giner, of *Hunt the Devil: A Demonology of US War Culture* (2015) and author of *Dissent from War* (2007) and *Democracy and America's War on Terror* (2005). His list of publications is available online at https://robertlivie.wordpress.com. He has served as editor of *Communication and Critical/Cultural Studies*, *Quarterly Journal of Speech*, and *Western Journal of Communication* and is a recipient of the National Communication Association's Distinguished Scholar Award.

INDEX

A

Aeschylus, 57n23
   Agamemnon, 44, 92–3, 97
   Prometheus Bound, 79n23–4
Agreda, María de, 83
America (hemispheric), 9, 20–5, 28–33, 133n62
American Legion, 42–3
Andrejevic, Mark, 52
angel, 10, 25, 48, 56, 77, 82–93, 95–7, 99–104
   Abraham's angels, 10, 82, 103, 122
   better angels, 10, 56, 77, 87–90, 108, 111, 130
   presence, 83, 86–7, 94, 101, 104, 128
   See also Gabriel, Michael, Raphael
   symbol of new awareness, 10, 83, 89
apocalypse, 53, 55
application, 94
archetype, 5, 64, 123
Ariel, 23–8, 32–3, 100–1, 103

Arrom, José Juan, 21
Arrowsmith, William, 104
authoritarianism, 3, 10, 51–2, 111, 115

B

Bacevich, Andrew J., 8, 70
Benjamin, Lee, 74
Beveridge, Albert, 46
Bird, Robert Montgomery, 42
Borges, Jorge Luis, 33, 82, 104
Boulding, Elise, 63
Burke, Kenneth, 33, 39–40, 52, 76–7, 96, 119
   comic corrective, 40, 44–5, 77, 97
   entelechy, 51–2
   perspective by incongruity, 76
   victimage ritual, 39–40, 51
Bush, George W., 18, 43, 46, 69, 79n39, 103, 113, 117
Butterworth, Michael, 7

C

Cady, Duane, 4
Caliban, 9, 21, 23–33, 93
Campbell, David, 7
Campbell, Joseph, 3
Caribbean, 21–2, 25, 29, 94
Césaire, Aimé, 25–8, 30, 32
Chappell, Paul, 73, 75–6
Cherniavsky, Eva, 111–5, 117
   disarticulated discourse, 113
   neocitizen, 111–2
Chernus, Ira, 2
Cohen, Richard, 46
coyote, 3–6, 9–10, 77, 110, 122, 130
Curtis, Tony, 42

D

Darío, Rubén, 23–4, 27
Darsey, James, 55
Deer, Patrick, 43
demagoguery, 10, 12n11, 32, 55, 59n58, 63, 109–10, 131n5
democracy, 2–4, 7–8, 10–12n4–5, 17–20, 24, 40–1, 51–2, 70, 98, 108–16, 123–4, 127–30
   democratic renewal, 11, 111, 115–6, 118, 120
   democratic self, 8, 20, 109, 129
   democratic space, 4, 10–11, 110–1, 118, 121–2, 129–30
   democratic values, 3, 109, 117, 121
   fugitive democracy109, 114–6, 122, 128, 130
   interdependence, 4, 10–11, 18, 109, 113–4, 118, 120, 129–30
   vigilant citizen, 114
   See also Ober, Joseph; Wolin, Sheldon
demonization, 12n11, 69, 110
Denton-Borhaug, Kelly, 2, 79n19
Dickinson, Emily, 87–9, 104
discourse, 2, 7–9, 11, 13, 16–21, 38, 41, 43, 50–2, 62–5, 73 100–1, 108–24, 128
   instability, 4, 62
   naturalized, 2, 4, 50, 62–3, 77n3
   dissent, 7, 11, 43–4, 51, 64–7, 71, 109–12, 126–30, 133n62
   deliberative dissent, 11, 109–10, 115–22, 130
   double gesture, 122
   premise of escape, 111
   See also peace (positive peace)
Dougherty, Kelly, 71
Douglas, Kirk, 42
Douglass, Frederick, 23, 29
Dow, Bonnie, 52
Dyson, Michael Eric, 3

E

Eliot, T.S., 103
empire, 2–4, 9–11, 20–56, 63, 77, 110, 127, 130
   after empire, 2–4, 7–9, 11, 77, 108
   imperial orthodoxy, 39, 110–1
   Roman empire, 41–2
   See also imperial warfare, war
Engels, Jeremy, 12n10
Englehardt, Tom, 2
Euripides, 44, 92, 102–4
evil, 1–2, 10, 16, 19–20, 43–52, 55–7, 65–9, 73, 87, 97, 99, 109, 125
exceptionalism, 1, 8–9, 16–20, 40–3, 51, 55, 63, 120, 129

F

Fast, Howard, 42
Fernández Retamar, Roberto, 26–8, 30
Ferner, Mike, 68–9
Fiala, Andrew, 8
Floyd, George, 120, 132n36
Forrest, Edwin, 41–2

INDEX

Frentz, Thomas S., 14n37
Frye, Northrop, 55

G

Gabriel, 10, 28, 82–4, 101
   annunciation, 83–4, 101
   crisis, 55, 86–7, 108, 122
   divestiture, 10, 85–7, 130
   illumination, 85–6
Gandhi, Mahatma, 63, 75
García Lorca, Federico, 82, 84
Genesio, Jerry, 66–7
God (Lord, Yahweh), 10, 22, 28, 31, 49–51, 67, 71, 74, 82–93, 95–7, 100–2
Gordone, Charles, 33
Greenberg, Karen J., 1

H

Haiti, 21–6, 29, 32, 35n21
Hansen, Lene, 63
Hartnett, Stephen, 7–8
Hasian, Marouf, Jr., 7, 9, 14n34
Hayes, Heather Ashley, 9
Heidt, Stephan, 9
Hiroshima, 102, 124
Hodges, Adam, 2, 62
Hughes, Richard, 55
Hussein, Saddam, 68–9, 126
Huston, John, 102
Hyde, Lewis, 3, 6

I

imperial warfare, 1, 46–8, 50–1, 120–3, 128–30
   heroic, 10, 41, 45, 48–50
   migratory, 10, 41, 48–9
   pristine, 10, 48–9
   routine, 48, 50
   rhythmic, 10, 41, 47
Islamic State, 45–51

J

Jacob's ladder, 84
Jekyll/Hyde duality, 86–7
Juana Inés de la Cruz, 33, 100
Jung, Carl, 50

K

Kennedy, John F., 42
Kennedy, Sheila, 9
Kierkegaard, Soren, 92–3, 95
King, Martin Luther, Jr., 28–9, 120
Kubrick, Stanley, 42
Kushner, Tony, 104

L

Laclau, Ernesto, 8, 114–8
   agonistic democracy, 114–6
   catachresis, 117–8
   contingency, 116–8
   liberal values, 117
   non-totalizing equivalence, 116, 118
   popular reason, 116–7
Lawrence, D.H., 8
Lederach, John Paul, 7
Lin, Maya, 98
Lincoln, Abraham, 10, 31, 87–92
Louverture, Toussaint, 22, 31–4

M

Marqués, René (*Sacrificio en el Monte Moriah*), 93–5, 97–104
Martí, José, 22–3, 25, 27–9, 40
Mary Magdalene, 71–2

Mary (mother of Jesus), 83–4, 101
McCain, John, 19
Meacham, Jon, 56
Mencken, H.L., 40–1
Mercieca, Jennifer, 52
Merton, Thomas, 87, 104
Michael (Archangel), 10, 82, 99–100
Musgrave, John, 99
Myth, 1–4, 6–11, 14n34, 16–9, 21–2, 26, 32–3, 36n41, 38–9, 41–3, 47–55, 62–6, 72–3, 76–7, 88, 93, 108–10, 114, 116, 122, 128, 130
    creative mythology, 3, 11
    mythology of war, 1
    warrior myth, 63–5, 76
    See also angel

N

Négritude, 25–6, 29–30, 32
Nelson, John, 64
Nietzsche, Friedrich, 39

O

Obama, Barack 9, 17–24, 28–33, 36n35, 35n41, 46–9, 53, 63
    Democratic presidential primary 2008, 16, 19
    Nobel Peace Prize speech, 16–9, 33
    presidential election campaign 2008, 16, 20
    prophetic voice, 10, 19, 65, 73
    rhetorical alchemy, 3, 6, 33, 86
    rhetorical juggler, 7–9, 17, 33
    speech at Democratic Party Convention 2004, 29
    speech at National Defense University, 47
    speech at West Point, 18–9
    speech on race, 30–1
    speech on Selma-to-Montgomery march, 20–1
    See also exceptionalism
Ober, Josiah, 111–12
oligarchy, 111, 114
Ortiz, Simon, 5
Orwell, George, 39
Osborn, Michael, 46
Ott, Brian, 53

P

Pagels, Elaine, 97
Pané, Ramon, 33
peace, 3–4, 7–8, 10, 16, 18–20, 43, 51, 62–5, 70, 73–6, 103, 110
    culture of peace, 3–4, 63, 67, 70, 121
    positive peace, 4, 17, 76, 120–2, 130
    waging peace, 10, 70, 75–7
Pease, Donald E., 8
Phillips, Kendall, 53
Philoctetes, 71, 80n50
Pincus, Walter, 49–50
Ponce, Aníbal, 27
productive criticism, 4, 13n17
prophecy, 3, 47, 52–3, 55, 64, 85
prosopopoeia, 11, 22–3, 126–9
Prospero, 9, 23–8, 30–4, 101
Puerto Rico, 35n25, 94–5, 98

R

racism, 4, 10, 70, 72–3, 120, 124
Raphael 10, 82, 89, 99
    atonement, 64, 91
    silence, 93, 95–9
    the satan, 3, 31, 96–7
redemptive violence, 19, 64
rhetoric, 7, 10–1, 39–40, 115–7, 123
    complementarity-hybridity-reflexivity, 18–9
    contingency, 116–8, 121, 130

See also productive criticism
Rice, Condoleezza, 103
ritual, 7, 10, 38–40, 46, 48–9, 51, 64, 95, 100, 108–9
Roberts-Miller, Patricia, 2, 12n11, 59n58
Rodó, José Enrique, 24–8
Roosevelt, Theodore, 46
Rushing, Janice Hocker, Rushing, 14n37

S

Seward, William, 88–9
Shakespeare, 11, 23–4, 26–8, 33, 88–91
    Hamlet, 88–91, 95
    King Lear, 106n26
    Macbeth, 47, 88, 91, 96
    Othello, 26, 88
    The Tempest, 23, 25–7, 30, 33, 100, 103
    See also Ariel, Caliban, Prospero
Sharma, Kriti, 118
Shaw, George Bernard, 106n16
Shi-xu, 9
similitude, 110, 117, 120–1
Simons, Jon, 43, 78n2
Slotkin, Richard, 8
Sodom and Gomorrah, 95, 100–3
soldier, symbol of, 64
Spartacus, 41–3
Stuckey, Mary, 52

T

Terrill, Robert, 52
terrorism, 1, 19, 45–54, 69, 76, 125, 128
Therese of Avila, St., 86
Thomson, Jeff, 5
trickster, 3, 6–7, 16, 41, 43–5, 76–7
tropes, 6, 8–9, 17–8, 54, 64, 76–7, 118–22, 129–30
    metaphor, 3, 8, 16, 39, 44, 51, 55–6, 76, 110, 119–20, 129
    metonymy, 119

irony, 110, 119, 123, 125, 129
synecdoche, 119
See also prosopopoeia
Trumbo, Dalton, 42
Trump, Donald, 10, 52–56, 111, 119
    demolition trope, 52–56
    rally rhetoric, 54
Twain, Mark, 40

V

veterans for peace, 66, 68, 120
    fact-finding mission to Nicaragua, 67–8
    humanizing the enemy, 68–9, 73, 110, 121, 127, 129, 130
    Iraq Veterans Against the War, 71–2
    Veterans For Peace position statements, 70
    Vietnam Veterans Against the War, 99
    Winter Soldier, 72, 80n51
Vico, 39, 76
Vidal, Gore, 91
Vietnam Veterans Memorial, 64, 98
vilification, 121–2

W

war, 1–4, 8–11, 16, 18, 22, 38–9, 44, 62, 65–6, 68, 70–5, 90, 103,124–5
    forever war, 1, 47
    Iraq War, 17, 43, 46, 48, 68–72, 103, 113
    just war, 8, 20, 49, 94, 123–4, 127
    militarism, 1–3, 8, 10, 18, 43, 49, 54, 62, 64–5, 70–7, 108, 120
    Spanish-American War, 23, 94
    U.S. Civil War, 1, 91, 98
    Vietnam war, 93, 98–9
    war culture, 2–4, 7, 9, 11, 12n7, 17–20, 43–5, 52, 57n16, 62–5, 76, 77n2, 79n19, 110, 119–23, 128–30
    World War II, 39, 123–5
    See also imperial warfare, Zinn, Howard

Wheatley, Phillis, 24
Whitman, Walt, 1, 20, 33, 42, 109
Williams, William Carlos, 8
Wolin, Sheldon, 56, 114–6, 118
Wright, Jeremiah, 30

Z

Zinn, Howard, 120, 122–9
   critique of the Good War, 123–5
   humanizing war's victims, 123, 125, 127, 129–30
   Iraq bombing, 126–7
   optimism, 129
   revisionist history, 123, 128
   Royan bombing, 125–6
   See also prosopopoeia

General Editors
Mitchell S. McKinney and Mary E. Stuckey

At the heart of how citizens, governments, and the media interact is the communication process, a process that is undergoing tremendous changes as we embrace a new millennium. Never has there been a time when confronting the complexity of these evolving relationships been so important to the maintenance of civil society. This series seeks books that advance the understanding of this process from multiple perspectives and as it occurs in both institutionalized and non-institutionalized political settings. While works that provide new perspectives on traditional political communication questions are welcome, the series also encourages the submission of manuscripts that take an innovative approach to political communication, which seek to broaden the frontiers of study to incorporate critical and cultural dimensions of study as well as scientific and theoretical frontiers.

For more information or to submit material for consideration, contact:

editorial@peterlang.com

To order other books in this series, please contact our Customer Service Department:

peterlang@presswarehouse.com (within the U.S.)
orders@peterlang.com (outside the U.S.)

Or browse online by series:

WWW.PETERLANG.COM

www.ingramcontent.com/pod-product-compliance
Lightning Source LLC
Chambersburg PA
CBHW061717300426
44115CB00014B/2726